FAMILY BUSINESS

Methods and Essentials of
Building Business Families

I0479639

MOHANAKRISHNAN RAMAN

INDIA · SINGAPORE · MALAYSIA

Notion Press

No. 8, 3rd Cross Street,
CIT Colony, Mylapore,
Chennai, Tamil Nadu – 600 004

First Published by Notion Press 2020
Copyright © Mohanakrishnan Raman 2020
All Rights Reserved.

ISBN 978-1-64983-849-0

This book has been published with all efforts taken to make the material error-free after the consent of the author. However, the author and the publisher do not assume and hereby disclaim any liability to any party for any loss, damage, or disruption caused by errors or omissions, whether such errors or omissions result from negligence, accident, or any other cause.

While every effort has been made to avoid any mistake or omission, this publication is being sold on the condition and understanding that neither the author nor the publishers or printers would be liable in any manner to any person by reason of any mistake or omission in this publication or for any action taken or omitted to be taken or advice rendered or accepted on the basis of this work. For any defect in printing or binding the publishers will be liable only to replace the defective copy by another copy of this work then available.

Contents

Acknowledgements

First and foremost, I would like to thank Mr. Santhiran, the Group Senior Director, at Mahsa University, Malaysia. He is the first one to put the seed in my mind and motivated me to write a book. I must recall Mr. Anthony Adaikalam, who is instrumental in meeting Mr. Santhiran in Mahsa University. I visited Brigham Young University in Provo, Utah in the USA, and met Prof. Gibb Dyer. Prof. Daniel Shanthakumar is the one took me to the University and created the opportunity to meet Prof. Gibb Dyer and my thanks are due to him. We had a long chat and decided to explore the possibilities of working together in some projects. Fortunately, when I started working on this book, he is the one guiding force, encouraging me to complete the book. He wrote a forward note as well for the book. I am highly indebted to his generosity and support for writing this book throughout. I thank John Adams Ph.D, Emeritus Professor of Organizational Systems at Saybrook University, for editing all the chapters and giving guidance to carry on this work. He took time in between his other commitments and supported this work, by sending edited chapters on time with his comments. My friend and Professor Balakrishnan Ramaswamy, who was also my English teacher in earlier years and a bilingual writer, is kind to spend lots of time in editing each chapter and involved until making the final manuscript. Without his continuous support and motivation, this book would not have been possible to be completed. My clients D. Venkateswaran, alias CD. Kumar, CD. Shanmugasundaram from CD group of companies, Erodu, Mr. C Devarajan, Managing Director of URC Group of Companies, Erodu, and Mr. R. Guru, past chairman of NR Group, Mysore, Mr. B. Soundararajan, Chairman of Suguna Foods, Coimbatore, who have readily agreed to share their experiences and gave permission to use their names and companies in the book while sharing the experiences and case studies.

My special thanks to Mr. Devarajan who readily agreed to support financially in bringing this book with the publisher. Last but not the least, I thank my wife Dr Bhavani M for compiling all references and helping to put it order. I must not miss to thank my children Nimesh. M (son), Sandhya. M, (daughter) and many of friends who have been a source of energy and motivation to complete this book.

More About the Author...

Raman Mohanakrishnan (Mohan) is an Industrial & Organizational Psychologist with Ph. D qualification. He has 22 years of wide-ranging experience in research, teaching, consulting, institution building projects and enjoys deep corporate exposure. He is passionate to contribute to higher education in management, social sciences and Organization Development Subjects.

He is currently holding position as

- Managing Director – Stepup Strategic Consulting Services Pvt Ltd (India)
- Managing Trustee – Foundation for Research, Education and Development (FRED)

He was a Professor and Head of HRD and OD department from SDM – IMD, Mysore from 2003 until 2008. He started an Educational Trust called Foundation for Research, Education and Development (FRED), to offer courses on Social & Behavioural Sciences including

OD, OB and Leadership. He had worked in Telecom, IT and Banking sectors. His corporate consulting areas *are **Family Business, OD Consulting, Innovation, Coaching and Organization Strategy.*** Training and Development being his forte, he has enormous interest in OD, and behavioural science- based training and interventions. He had done Competency Mapping through Development Centre process for more than 1500 managers in a large private bank, as a part of major change management project in India. His *strategy and OD consulting* assignments include organizations in Construction, FMCG, Manufacturing, Education, Banking and IT sectors. He has been an invited speaker in various forums like CII, NIPM, IFTDO, ATDO, ISODC and IODA.

He has done more than 250 development workshops for various clients. He also has designed and offered open programs in the areas of Talent Management, Performance & Career Management Systems & Process and *Personal Transformation* Clinic to say a few. He was instrumental and offered leadership in organizing Global Organization Development Summit (GODS) in the year 2006, and as a result he was instrumental in Founding Asia OD Network (AODN), along with other notable OD leaders. He was a Founder President of AODN for three years from 2007 to 2009. He had spearheaded and offered his leadership to the GODS in China in 2007 and 2008 in Thailand. Under his leadership GODS was organized again in 2009 and 2016 in India.

He has published a paper in well reputed European journal "Challenging Organizations and Society" 2014, Volume 3, Issue 2, titled "The Caste System in India – its Power in Organizations and Politics". He also contributed articles/chapters in edited books.

He had served as the **Vice President – Conferences and Events** (2016-19) for International Organization Development Association (IODA). He served as an Executive Board Member of IODA since 2007 to help the conference organizing teams in IODA across the world.

He was consultant with Integrated Consulting Group (ICG) Austria and involved in *"Innovation Boot Camp"* creating an innovation culture at the various ministerial departments of the countries of *Finland and Estonia.* He was invited to give a motivational and directional speech in the area of *"Smart Specialization" (Innovation project) for the Government of Slovenia*

He was a visiting professor at the School of Psychology in Zurich University of Applied Science (ZHAW), Switzerland for the last few years from 2015. He is recognized as an **Erasmus Professor** to teach in Slovenia by the Education Ministry of Education, Slovenia. He has guided, coached and mentored many European Business Consultants and Executives. He has also delivered keynote speeches and workshops in China. His specialization in coaching is cross-national consonance.

His other interests are travel, Wildlife and Environment Conservation. He was a Dean – Academics & OD for a large Educational institution in Mysore, India from 2016-2018. He is a TiE Mysore Chapter Charted Member.

Foreword

In this new book, *Family Business: Methods and Essentials of Building Business Families*, Dr Mohanakrishnan Raman, provides the reader with theories and models to understand the dynamics of family business in Asia. This is a unique contribution since most of the research and consulting practice regarding family business has been written by Western scholars, thus we know little about the dynamics of Asian family firms. Dr. Raman provides the reader with a basic overview of the family dynamics in a variety of Asian countries—China, Japan, India, Malaysia, Indonesia, etc., which provides the context for us to understand how family businesses function in these countries. While there is variance in family dynamics in Asia, Dr. Raman points out how most families are patriarchal in nature, with the eldest family member given respect and the right to make many family decisions. Women are generally in a subservient role and have a difficult time contributing to a family business in a meaningful way. Thus, there is a tension in

Asian family businesses regarding gender that needs to be managed effectively if Asian women will have the opportunity to contribute to family businesses.

Dr. Raman also helps the reader understand the basic values that underpin Asian family businesses. These values which are embedded in Asian culture provide the rules of conduct for family business members and shape the kinds of behaviors and outcomes that we see in Asian family firms. Values such as "love" and "gratitude" are seen by Dr. Raman as essential for a family firm to succeed over time and creating norms of reciprocity where family members feel obligated to help one another is seen as essential. The importance of creating a "family vision" that is connected with the creation of a "family business constitution" is described in detail. Such a document provides the rules of behavior that will govern the family and the firm and provides a focus for family goals and positive outcomes. Succession planning is the key to continuity in family business and Dr. Raman provides the reader with the steps that a family business needs to succeed over time. This is probably the most important chapter in the book for family business leaders. How to govern the firm effectively is another important issue to be managed by family business leaders. The book highlights the challenges in creating an effective family governance system and suggests ways to improve governance in family firms. One of the most important chapters in the book concerns "health and wellness." This is a relatively unexplored topic in family business, and Dr. Raman helps family business leaders understand the importance of health to the family business and how to improve the health of family business members.

The book is filled with examples of Dr. Raman's experiences in consulting with family businesses. These case examples help the reader understand how a consultant can help a family business and they highlight the dynamics of family firms that Dr. Raman has observed in his extensive consulting practice. In summary, this book is a must read for all family business leaders, researchers, and consultants who are interested in improving Asian family businesses. I highly recommend it.

Dr. W. Gibb Dyer,
O. Leslie and Dorothy C. Stone Professor
Marriott School of Business,
Brigham Young University
August 3, 2020

Introduction

Family Business or Business Families

I was suggested in random to write a book on family business by Mr. Santhiran, the Group Director of Marketing, Mahsa University, Malaysia. His suggestion came as a surprise and at the same time, I realized his words touched my deep desire to write a book on family business. I have been in consulting work for the last one and half decades apart from academic and corporate experience. The book on Consulting to Family Businesses by Jane and Dyer (2003) was my first inspiration to start thinking on family business consulting. I had the opportunity to meet Prof. Gibb Dyer, Jr last year at Brigham Young University, Provo, Utah, US. We discussed the possibilities of collaborating in the field to write, offer programs and consulting. Mr. Santhiran's suggestion came at the right time to motivate me to start writing on family business, based on knowledge gathered through my readings on the topic, consulting experiences with few families in India and reflections on learning in the field. It wasn't easy to start writing a book as I have to plan the flow of the topics, chapters, case studies and many other things. I am an abstract thinker and good in connecting dots, offering creative solutions to the client systems. However, I have written only few articles so far in contributing to book chapters and couple of publications. When I agreed to write a book, I know I am committing to a task for which I need to gain energy and focus in the new habit which I want to pursue, putting things in more organized manner. However, I was determined and give complete attention, focus and energy to complete this piece of work as I just completed a talk in you tube on the topic of "Discipline". The words and my own explanations in the video were ringing in years and motivated me to start working on this book. I am sure with the experience what I had, and my ability to articulate while speaking to my clients, would definitely add value for the readers.

The topic of Family Business in last couple of decades has become a hot topic in Business schools and corporate circles as many family owned businesses came to limelight. The reasons are being that they are listed in the stock markets (Reliance Group), known for successful leadership changes within the family (Rahul Bajaj), professionalizing the management (Murugappa Group), and making inroads into international markets (HCL).

There are several books on family business, written over last five decades. It is highly complex to collate the topics of all these books and identify what each of the authors was trying to offer it as knowledge or depictions of concerned areas. But in general, through topic analysis of the contents of the books, I realized that most of the authors were offering the knowledge content in the topics of Succession Planning, Family Conflict Resolution, Family Wealth and Asset Management, Estate Management, Family Governance and setting Family Constitution Policies. On the other hand, I found that not much focus was given to the most important areas such as, Business Hand Over Process to the NextGen, Retirement Plans, Policies and Roles for the elders, Love, Values, Gratitude, Forgiveness, Family Health in particular were, and more.

Therefore, I have decided that I will cover topics which are common to the family businesses and emphasize on the areas which are not given great importance in the literature. At the same time, I would keep this book, kind of an academic one and not a theoretical one explaining complex frameworks and models. I would prefer this book as a complete model or a guidance book. I want family members to read this, choose the topics as they wish or in need and understand what they should do the next.

This book will throw light on the areas of importance for the family business on commonly confronting issues. The chapter wise plan goes as I explain in the following paragraphs.

Chapter One: It deals with an understanding of what is a family? The succeeding generations must understand the importance of family and cannot be allowed to be complacent. It is from my experience especially that third generation onwards there is a tendency to feel that "I have all" and "I can do anything". However, the preceding generations worry about such an attitude and have no clue on how they manage the succeeding generations. In other words, they have no knowledge on how to bring the next generation through succession and what they should do before they have the plan of succession planning. The chapter one deals with giving a proper introduction of what is family and how important family is, how family is a resource and an asset. Family is a capital according to Dyer (2019). I have also given other content also in the following:

Chapter Two: It deals with Family Values & Vision. Values that are the key differentiators, for the individuals, families, and in large for the tribes and societies. I try to narrate the importance and core values in this book for the business families and sustain them for generations, though values themselves are volatile over the years as they change generation to generation. However, certain core values are the clear differentiators for family businesses and the family firm is identified with the values they practice for centuries. The core values, terminal & instrumental values, moral values are discussed for the benefit of the readers. Values play a major role in building culture and institutions. Understanding of instrumental and terminal values, moral values and personal conduct & behaviors are the keys to successful transition from generation to generation. On the other hand, Vision Building, is a key component of forming the family members where the family wants to go or reach even after the generations. Consensus with all family members to achieve its primary goals in terms of business and family are the most important factors. The six steps for vision building and strategy by Steve Miller explains how the process of building vision can be achieved.

Chapter Three: This chapter is an important contribution from me as an author of this book. In my consulting experience, especially when I deal with conflicts among the family members, I never had a weapon of positive disposition in nature. We have been taught to use the models of conflict resolution and negotiation. I thought we need an enhanced practice that can even diffuse high potential negative conflicts. When I searched for such materials or tools, I found not much or no useful stuff in family business research and literature but found few beautifully written articles in family therapy domain. I took the cues to build this chapter along with what I am thinking on the topics of reciprocity. When I introduced reciprocity as a practicing tool or habit, family members thanked me for this new thinking. This chapter, I am sure readers would enjoy and find it really useful to practice in their families to strengthen the relationships further. The reciprocity to love and expression and gratitude will return with unbelievable results.

Chapter Four: I deal with succession planning and handing over course of action (Inheriting the Mantle) of family business. Many family business members and executives must have read enormous number of articles and also would have attended several workshops to understand the dynamics and challenges in designing a succession planning for the next generation. I have attended a few conferences in family business areas and I found there are lots of anxiety and uncertainty, in some cases lots of frustration from the succeeding generations when the current governing generation do not hand over the business with the faith that next generation will run it profitably or efficiently. This chapter contributes to the readers that it is not only succession planning, which is important, but it is also important to prepare the elder generation to hand over and create a plan for the retirement.

Chapter Five: Writing Family constitution is another topic, which has several complications as many business families assume that everything will be run smoothly, and their offspring will take care of themselves. I know of families where even a will was not written and after the demise of the father, the families have collapsed due to legal complications over inheritance of business and wealth. Though writing a family constitution is not a panacea to all problems, but it lays a rule for all family members to come on one page and realize the potential use of the same. It is built and written in consensus with each of the family members and lays the rules for the family and implementation. It lays rules on many potential conflict areas such as succession planning, dividends, education, estate management, policies for the family and much more. The chapter gives a comprehensive idea on how the constitution can be written and implemented.

Chapter Six: Running a family together as one single unit with varied interests and capabilities among its members can easily defocus the business interests and also can create a potential conflict. Family governance practice or documenting it makes the difference to the families on its setting goals, arriving at consensus, making decision and communication among all the stakeholders. From the simple to complex situations based on the family size is being discussed in detail here and the processes of bringing alignment and practice are also given.

Chapter Seven: Family health and wellness is a new topic. When I started this book, the covid-19 pandemic was at peak in its first wave and many of my clients are worried about the future of business and their families including me. I found only one article in my search on family health was written by Prof. Peter Vogel from IMD, Switzerland. I contacted him to republish his work for which he readily agreed and used his article as a starting point. I reproduced the whole article and then wrote the chapter, need and importance of health and wellness in family businesses. In fact, I would confidently state that chapter three on reciprocity and chapter seven are my original contributions to this book and rest of the topics have a plethora of reading materials available in many platforms.

Summary

I hope the content, the list of topics in it must give an inspiration for the reader to enjoy the book and learn accordingly from it. This is the initial attempt in my career as a consultant which should serve the reader an additional tool to assimilate with me in training sessions. People can also learn from it independently, otherwise, the content and context may give necessary information about family business.

Chapter 1

What is Family and Family Business?

Introduction

This book is all about family business. There are many businesses which are carried on by generations, passing it over from father to son and the like ...this is mostly understood as a business family sometimes involving more members like the cousins, brothers and others too, based on their interests and family interests.

In other words, it is also, how family members involve in a business in securing wealth and their intention to pass the wealth and business to the succeeding generations within the family not giving an opportunity to others. There are examples of businesses belonging to families, which are more than 300 years old. This chapter deals with an understanding of what families are. It lays a foundation for understanding the next chapters from the familial perspective on managing businesses. The succeeding generations must understand the importance of family and cannot be allowed to be complacent. In my experience, especially from the third generation in a wealthy family and beyond as well, there is a tendency to feel that "I have it all" and "I can do anything". However, the preceding generations worry about such an attitude and have no clue about how to manage the succeeding generations. In other words, they have no knowledge of how to bring the next generation through succession, and what they should do before complete planning on who to succeed and how to succeed. This chapter develops a proper introduction of what a family is, how important the family is, and how the family is both a resource and an asset. Family "*is capital*" according to Dyer (2019)[1]. He further explains that the family comes with three kinds of resources such as Family Human Capital, Family Social Capital and Family Financial Capital. The next generations are the beneficiaries of capitals mentioned and use these resources.

The Origin of the Word Family

In the early 15[th]century, the word "famila", in the Latin language, meant "servants of a household". The word "*familia*"included the servants in the household, all the "members of the household, the estate, and property of the household, including relatives and servants,"

The Latin word rarely appears in the sense "parents with their children,"

However, the derivatives of *famulus* include several related words such as "*famula*" serving woman or maid, "*famulanter*" in the manner of a servant, "*famulitas*" servitude, "*familiaris* " of one's household, private," *familiaricus* "of household slaves, and " *familiaritas,* "close friendship."

Later in 15th Century, in English, "family" was defined as a sense of "collective body of persons who form one household under one head and one domestic government, including parents, children, and servants, and as sometimes used, even lodgers or boarders" [Century Dictionary]. From the 1660s,it meant "parents with their children, whether they dwell together or not," also in a more general sense, "persons closely related by blood, including aunts, uncles, and cousins." Earlier, it was "those who descend from a common progenitor, a house, a lineage" (1580s). Hence, "any group of things classed as kindred based on common distinguishing characteristics" (1620s); as a scientific classification, between genus and order, from 1753.

Family – Understanding the Basics

We need to understand the anthropological and sociological perspectives in family formation. These sciences throw light on different ways as such how the families are being formed and lived for long years, until now. They further depict the reflections of it with different types of families and how each influences its family members on development, and of their values, vision and mission building, especially in the family business practice. The explanations and definitions of families have deep roots in anthropological and sociological theories, which we will see in detail in next paragraphs.

Families are defined based on the types of marriages and the relationships between men and women. In this context let us explore different family practices in the paragraphs that follow. Based on the understandings of the types of families, the value formation and vision building are explained, for family businesses.

Family An Institution

Throughout this book let me talk about the issue of families in the context of business families or family businesses. Hence understanding an idea of family and getting the knowledge on family, how it is being formed and how it thrives, create awareness among the family members who constantly think for family, family development and creation of wealth for the family. I personally always think that having a sound platform and understanding of an issue or topic gives the way for emergence of clarity and application of this rationale.

The family is the most important primary group in a society[2]. It is the simplest and the most elementary form of society. The family as an institution is universal. It is the most permanent and the most pervasive of all social institutions. In case of the west, family is defined as an economic and social unit. In case of India, China and Japan, family is a cultural religious unit. Sociologists have spoken of different forms or types of family. Different sociologists have different ways to illustrate the family types.

In order to understand the way the families are being formed, it is necessary to understand how the sociologists explain the family system and its formation. Polygamous societies still exist in northern Africa and East Asia (Altman and Ginat 1996)[3]. Instances of polygamy are almost exclusively in the form of polygamy. Polygamy refers to a man being married to more than one woman at the same time. The reverse, when a woman is married to more than one man at the same time, is called polyandry. It is far less common and only occurs in about 1 percent of the world's cultures (Altman and Ginat 1996)[3]. Based on Polygamy, Polygyny or Polyandry, there are different types of families that can be understood: Matriarchal Family, Patriarchal Family, Nuclear Family and Joint Family.

Types of Families

Matriarchal Family

This may have roots in the practice of polyandry. The matriarchal family functions as a mother centered or mother dominated family. Usually the mother or the woman heads the family, and she has complete authority and manages the wealth. Daughters gain more attention and have the legal heir status or inherit the wealth of the mother. The matriarchal family is matrilocal in residence; which means that the wife stays back in her mother's home after marriage. The husband lives or makes occasional visits to the wife's home. But in practice, some relatives of the family, such as her brother, exercise authority in the family. The maternal family brings together the kinsmen the members of a family who is blood related and welds them in a powerful group.

Patriarchal Family

The patriarchal family is also known as father centered or father dominated family. The father is the head of the family and exercises authority. He is the administrator of the family property. Descent, inheritance, and succession are recognized through the male line. Patriarchal families are patrilineal in character because the descent is traced through the male line. Only the male children inherit the property. The Patriarchal family is patrilocal in residence. Sons continue to live with the father in his own house even after their marriages. Only the wives come and join them. Women have secondary positions in these families. Children are brought up in their father's family.

Nuclear Family

The individual nuclear family is a universal social phenomenon. It can be defined as a small group composed of husband and wife and children that constitute a unit apart from the rest of the community. They live in their own home and not in either of their parents' homes. The nuclear family is a characteristic feature of all the modern industrial societies in which a high degree of structural and functional specialization exists. The nuclear family comprises a cohabiting man and woman who maintain a socially approved sexual relationship and have at least one child. The traditional nuclear family is a nuclear family in which the wife works in the home without pay while the husband works outside the home for money.

Joint Family

The joint family is also known as undivided family or extended family. It normally consists of members belonging to two or three generations: husband and wife, their married and unmarried children and their married or unmarried grandchildren. The joint family system constituted the basic social institution in many traditional societies', particularly Asian societies like the Indian society. The joint family is a mode of combining smaller families into larger family units through the extension of three or more generations. In a joint family the members are related through blood and spread over several generations, living together under a common space and work under a common head.

Marriage as an Institution

The word family has very interesting explanations and roots from the 15th century in the western world, it is also important for us to know the different ways families are being formed when there is an agreement between a man and a woman to marry and live as spouses or couple and produce children. Different cultures practice different ways of accepting or has rule of a marriage between a man and woman. For an example, in many western societies, which have evolved over many years, any adult man or woman can choose to live together with an opposite sex. They may decide go get married or they may continue to live together, even to produce children. In western societies, it is purely the decision of an adult to marry anyone he or she chooses, irrespective of race, religion, or social status. They develop courtship and then marry legally or continue to live together.

However, in Asian countries, marriages are not this simple. In a country like India, there are very stringent norms for marriages, even after a son or daughter has become an adult and is self-sufficient in terms of earning. The family decides whom one should marry based on religion, caste, and wealth. The dowry system is very common and it still prevails, even though there is a strict law to protect Indian women in marriage.

Other Asian countries also practice different ways and methods of a marriage. It is important for the reader to understand the many differences among Asian families. The following paragraphs will explore some of those belief systems and cultural differences.

I will include a few Asian countries for the understanding of the reader of this book, with reference to the families that are found in these nations and their similarities in terms of appearance. Common family themes across these nations are the "bondage" of relationship. The working system of families and the male oriented dominance in Asian families, including Chinese, Japanese, Korean, Vietnamese, Cambodian, Indian and Indonesian families are somewhat similar. One thing that is important to understand is the range of diversity in family "operation". It is most interesting to understand that diversity between and within these groups in terms of history, language, religious practices, occupation and demographic variables. The most pronounced belief in Asian culture, except in the Filipino, Indian, Pakistani and Bangladeshi cultures, is the *Confucian* value system, largely coming from China. This code of conduct determines the relationships an individual has with people, and their obligations to others (obey your parents, be a good citizen, and take care of your family). However, those nations following other than the Confucian Value System also have similar values when it comes to gender inequality. In a nutshell, most of Asian nations are predominantly male dominated or Patriarchal in nature.

Chinese families: The Chinese family is the product of social, legal, political, and economic factors interacting with culture through generations of families (Morrison Wong, 1988)[4]. The majority of Asian families can trace their roots to the traditional family structure of China, which includes (1) *patriarchal rule,* with clearly defined roles of male dominance; (2) *patrilocal residence patterns,* where married couples lived with the husband's parents; and (3) *extended families*; in which many generations lived with their offspring under one roof.

The traditional Chinese family places the utmost importance on roles which are prescribed by the culture. These roles are defined by hierarchy, obligation, and duty. The family is thought of as a collective unit. An individualistic perspective is not generally an acceptable one and is seen as disruptive and disrespectful to the family. Marriages are commonly arranged, and spousal relationships are secondary to parent-child relationships. Males within the Chinese culture are dominant, and fathers handle familial disciplinarian responsibilities. On the other hand, women are affectionate, self-sacrificing, and caring as mothers; taught to assist with household responsibilities as daughters; and adhere to the *thrice-obeying* rule such as comply with 1) father or eldest brother in their youth, 2) husbands in marriage, 3) and sons when she is widowed. (Tung 2000)[5]. In my personal quest to understand different cultures and practices, during my teaching, and also in organizing a conference at Shenyang Jianzhu University in China, in the year 2007, as well my travel to the cities of Beijing and Shanghai to deliver keynote speeches at some conferences, I learned from local professional colleagues that Chinese woman are expected to learn five important skills; to play a musical instrument, to sing, and to do traditional dancing, cooking and sewing. This practice is not welcomed by these women any longer, as the ratio of females to males dwindled due to the one child policy.

Because of the emphasis of ancestor worship, having sons to carry on the family name and serving in-laws are also cherished values. Another important value is *filial piety*; family relations are characterized by duty, obligation, importance of the family name, self-sacrifice for the good of the elders, and respect for status (Williams-Leon and Nakashima 2001)[6].

Japanese families: Japan, which has gone through a difficult period after the world war II, became successful economically, and at this time, the Japanese economy stands the third best in terms of GDP growth with 4.97 trillion as per the International Monetary Fund Survey (2020)[7]. However, Japan is always viewed as one of the cultures which didn't dilute its value systems and used it for its supremacy in production, quality and business. The Japanese family assigns responsibility based on gender. Women are considered as carriers, and transmitters, of tradition. Women handle most of the household work, childcare and child rearing. Men, on the other hand, are expected to provide financial comforts for the family.

The Japanese are taught to never be individualistic, but rather to be a good as a team member or belong to a group. In other words, the Japanese are taught to be conscious of others all the time, rather than giving importance to self and never expressing an inclusive, independent attitude.

Korean families: Korean families are also hierarchical in nature. They practice hierarchy by gender, generation, age, and class. There is differentiation between women and men; woman has traditional gender roles, like Chinese and Japanese families. Parents support children until they settle down. In turn, the children are obligated to respect their parents.

Jip-an, which means *"within the house,"* identifies family membership, values, and traditions practiced within a family. Marriage in Korean culture is considered as a union among families rather than two individuals coming together. (Coleman and Steinhoff 1992)[8]. Prior to marriage, the family's community standing, social status, wealth and other aspects are considered as well as the specific credentials of the family members.

Vietnamese families: China deeply influenced Vietnam's culture before the French occupied Vietnam. The early history of this region shows different groups of people living under the shadow of the powerful empire of China. Even when the Vietnamese gained independence in 1945, the rulers maintained the use of Chinese governance systems and culture.

The elite upper classes were vastly influenced by Chinese culture, lifestyle, food, language, and Confucianism in Vietnam.

Vietnam adopted Chinese Confucianism enthusiastically, and the code of conduct was used to govern its society for centuries. Like many other Asian cultures, the Vietnamese hold elders in high regard, and respect their position in the family. Both adults and children are taught to remain quiet when elders are in conversations and to listen with great intent of respect. Eye contact is seen as disrespectful and shaking hands with both hands is considered as respectful.

Vietnamese families expect the rules of etiquette to be followed. Marriages are arranged by parents or by the young couple's own initiative. Once married, the union is considered permanent unless the woman commits adultery. Until the mid-1950s, adultery by men was overlooked, unless the position of the wife was in jeopardy in the extended family or children were not guaranteed financial security.

In traditional Vietnamese families, the husband is the head of the family, chief financial provider, and the rest of the family looks to him for guidance. The wife is the caregiver and comforter of the family and only deals with the outside community by choice (Trinh 2002)[9].

Cambodian families: Present day Cambodia has the history of the amazing Khmer dynasty, which ruled Cambodia for several centuries and was influenced by Tamil-Buddhism philosophies. They also went through a very difficult period during the "Khmer Rouge" period, wherein more than 1.5 million people were killed. The country is still reeling under these experiences. Cambodians live with the famous proverb "Fear not the future, weep not for the past". Life in Cambodia has been gradually improving since the 1990s economically, due to support from Vietnam and other countries. The Cambodian population is a racial mix of indigenous tribal people (Khmer), Chem., Chinese and Indians. Unlike many of the neighboring countries, the majority of the people are Buddhists with a small Muslim population. The Cambodian family is based on close relationships (extended kin). Central values within the Cambodian family are built around harmony and balance (Sun-Him 1987)[9].

The husband is considered the head of the household and always expects to be consulted prior to decision making. Women in Cambodian culture hold stereotypical subordinate gender roles within the family (Sun-Him 1987)[10].

Indonesian families: Indonesia is one of the largest Muslim nations, with over 90 percent of the population belonging to the Islamic Faith. There are over 100 distinct groups in Indonesia, each with its own cultural identity in relation to language, class, customs, and values. In the Indonesian family, family closeness and loyalty, obligation, and respect for parents is important (Collins and Bahar 1995)[11].

Indonesian culture emphasizes that it is the responsibility of the male to generate income for the family's welfare. Muslim men in Indonesia may have a maximum of four wives, but few do, because the husband must secure the permission from previous wives and treat each equally.

Women are taught to respect their husbands and are the primary caretakers of the family; women are responsible for domestic maintenance. Children are taught to obey and respect their parents. It is also common for children to remain in the homes of their parents for extended lengths of time. In fact, it has been reported that most young Indonesian individuals live with either their parents or extended family until they marry (Collins and Bahar 1995).[11].

Malaysian Families: Malaysian families are generally collectivist in nature. Everyone sees every individual in the family as one. Therefore, the individuals from the family must be cautious and conscious about how they behave in social settings. The family has the authority to supersede the interest of the individual members. Malaysian families are patriarchal in nature, and the father is generally the head of the family. All elders are respected and consulted before any major decisions such as marriages or investments are made.

The links Malaysian people maintain with their extended families overseas are much closer than those maintained by most extended families in Western societies. However, some members of the younger generation have become less family orientated.

In Chinese-Malaysian households, *"filial piety"* is displayed at all times. The women's roles usually carry out the domestic chores, taking care of children and household.

Indian Families: Indian families[12] often consist of three to four living generations, sometimes also including uncles, aunts, nieces, nephews and grandparents. The head of the family is generally the senior male family member and is respected for his age and experience. The head of the family sets up the rules for the family. Usually, the head of the family manages the finances, assets, and wealth. He serves as the judge in case of family disputes and plays a strong role in conflict resolutions among the family members.

The Joint Family System of India: There are strong traditions of Indian joint family systems, which everyone is expected to, accept and follow. A young male should always touch the feet of his elders in order to receive the elder's blessings; he should never speak in a high or rude tone to those who are older than him; he should always give respect to elders, and he should not drink alcohol and tobacco or smoke cigarettes in front of them; he should respect women. Girls are not allowed to wear skirts after they reach a certain age, while in others, they can wear saris, or other traditional attire, as long as it is decent and not body-revealing.

Traditionally, complete joint families always lived together, and they eat the food cooked at one fireplace and are linked to one another through family relationship bonds. All members share a common source of income generated by the earning family member. An Unemployed member of the family is helped by their parents or other earning members. Children grow up in close contact with their aunts, uncles, grandparents, and cousins.

One of the important characters of the joint family is its *give and take* nature. Family tasks like cooking, cleaning, caring for the children, and performing home maintenance are structured in a collective manner. The family members complete the tasks on a rotating basis, or else individual family members become responsible for specific tasks. Every family member involves and participates in life-cycle events or celebration such as births, marriages, deaths, and all types of annual or regional festival celebrations.

Position of Males and Females in Society

Males are preferred more than females in Indian society; they are given more value than women in the family across the society. Males are independent, self-reliant, demanding, and domineering. Other hand, females are quiet, helpful, selfless, and conservative and dependent. Naturally an Indian woman always must depend on somebody throughout her life; in childhood, she depends on her father, in married life, she depends on her husband, and in older years, she depends on her son.

In a traditional Indian family, the wife is typically dependent, submissive, obedient, modest, nonassertive, and goes out of her way to please her husband. Women are entrusted with the responsibility of looking after the home and caring for the children plus elderly parents and relatives.

Evolving Family Systems in India

Today we have a generation of people, who after having lived in a joint family system, have more and more frequently decided to break out and have their own nuclear families. The generation that broke out of the old joint family system did so when personal thinking began to gain predominance in the society, during the last three decades.

Another factor that creates nuclear families is profession. This forced men and women to move out of their families for better job opportunities. This often means departing to the major commercial cities and towns. In this case, often the parents who remain emotionally attached to the place where they spent most of their lives preferred to continue staying in their family home and accepted with some sadness their children starting out new lives away from them.

The nuclear family gave immense freedom from the traditions and ways of life that the old system was characterized by. The one and only major gain that we see from the 'nuclear family' system is the opportunity it provides everyone to create an identity of their own.

Families and Family Business

The learning from the above paragraphs makes understand the way the families try to strive and sustain. The families when they start working for making ways for their living in the world of economics prefer to do some work such as, engage in labor for wages, involve in trading goods, start manufacturing of goods, and in many other avocations. In the context of this book we are more interested in learning about families which involve in business and how they sustain the business for long time and hand it over to other generations. Let's look at what is family business and understand it better that will give us the platform to learn about the many topics in family business through the subsequent chapters.

A family-owned business may be defined "as any business in which two or more family members are involved and the majority of ownership or control lies within a family". Family-owned businesses may be the oldest form of business organization. Farms were an early form of family business in which what we think of today as the private life and work life were intertwined. In urban settings, it was once normal for a shopkeeper or doctor to live in the same building in which he or she worked, and family members often helped with the business as needed.

A family business can be described as an interaction between two separate but interdependent systems—the business and the family—with uncertain boundaries and different rules. Graphically, this concept can be presented as two intersecting circles. Family businesses may include numerous combinations of family members in various business roles, including husbands and wives, parents and children, extended families, and multiple generations playing the roles of stockholders, board members, working partners, advisors, managers, and employees. Conflicts often arise due to these overlapping roles. The ways in which individuals typically communicate within a family may be inappropriate in business situations. Likewise, personal concerns or rivalries may carry over into the workplace to the detriment of the firm. In order to succeed, a family business must keep its lines of communication open, make use of strategic planning tools, and engage the assistance of outside advisors as needed. In order to understand these dynamics better it is very important to know the research carried out by Renato Tagiri and John Davis in the early 1980s[13].

The Three-Circle Model of the Family Business System was developed as a conceptual model by Renato Tagiuri and John Davis (1996)[13]at Harvard Business School is a significant contribution to the field of family business for understanding the interactions among the three important elements which are interdependent and overlapping namely; Ownership, Business, and Family. In their article Bivalent Attributes of the Family Firm mentions that "family company has several unique, inherent attributes, and each of these attributes are source of benefits and disadvantages for owning families, nonfamily employees, and family employees".

The Three Circle Model[14]

The model proposed by Taguri and Davis (1982)

The Three Circle System as Explained by John Davis

An individual in a family business system occupies one of the seven sectors that are formed by these three overlapping circles. An owner (partner or shareholder) and *only* an owner will sit within the top circle. Family members will occupy the left-hand circle, and employees of the family company in the right-hand circle. If you have only one of these roles, you will be in just one circle. However, if you have two roles, you will be in an overlapping sector, sitting within two circles at one time. If you are a family member who works in the business but has no ownership stake, you're in the bottom-center sector. If you are a family member who works in the business and is a proprietor, then you will sit right in the center of the three overlapping circles.

"The Model identifies where key people are located in the system," Davis explains, "and think about different roles that family members have: being a family owner, or a family employee. These overlap areas in the Model indicate role overlaps and potential role confusion."

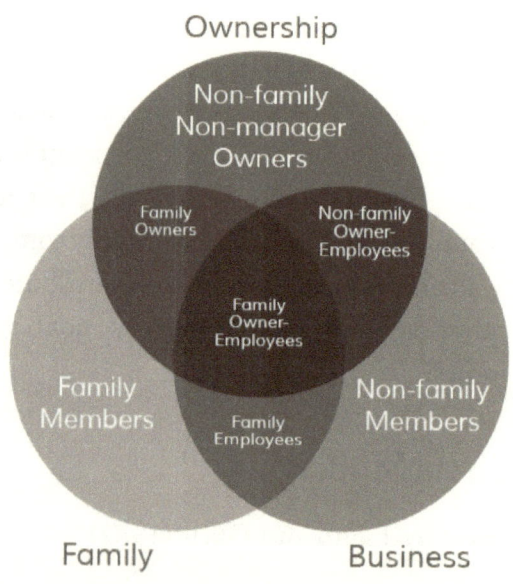

Each of the seven interest groups identified by the Model has its own viewpoints, goals, concerns, and dynamics. The Model reminds us that the views of each sector is legitimate and deserve to be respected. No one viewpoint is more legitimate than another, but the different viewpoints must be integrated in order to set future direction for the family business system. The long-term success of family business systems depends on the functioning and mutual support of each of these groups.

With the Three-Circle Model, one can depict seven distinct interest groups (or stakeholders) with a connection to the family business:

1. Family members not involved in the business, but who are descendants or spouses/partners of owners.

2. Family owners not employed in the business.

3. Non-family owners who do not work in the business.

4. Non-family owners who work in the business.

5. Non-family employees.

6. Family members who work in the business but are not owners.

7. Family owners who work in the business.

The notion, FAMILY BUSINESS becomes more interesting, when we apply the three-circle model and the seven different types of interest groups for our understanding. It is also portraying the complexity in managing the family and business.

Summary

This chapter is presented with an objective of making the reader to get familiar with the etymology of the word family and traced its significance of anthropological and sociological perspectives. The types of families which are described for knowing various ways the families operate live and sustain. The book wanted to emphasize the perspectives of the Asian region and the cultural influence from various countries within Asia. Hence, different countries and its national culture and its influence of the families are also described. Finally, with all these backgrounds when a family turns out to be a business family or a family business how the family business is looked at for understanding and clarity. The complexity of multiple roles and interests are explained through the three-circle model.

References

1. Dyer, W. G. (2019), *"The family edge: How your biggest competitive advantage in business isn't what you've been taught—it's your family"*. Sanger, CA: Familius.

2. https://www.sociologyguide.com/marriage-family-kinship/Types-of-the-family.php

3. Altman et al., (1996), *Polygamous Families in Contemporary Society*. New York: Cambridge University Press

4. Wong, M. G. (1988), *"The Chinese American Family."* in ethnic Families in America, Ed. C. Mindel, R. W. Habenstein, and R. Wright, Jr. New York: Elsevier.

5. Tung, M. P. M. (2000), *"Chinese Americans and their Immigrant Parents: Conflict, Identity, and Values"*. Binghamton, NY: Haworth Press.

6. Williams-Leon, T., and Nakashima, C. L. (2001). *The Sum of our Parts: Mixed Heritage of Asian Americans. Philadelphia"*: Temple University Press.

7. International Monetary Fund Survey – 2020. https://blogs.imf.org/2020/04/14/the-great-lockdown-worst-economic-downturn-since-the-great-depression/

8. Coleman, S. J. and Steinhoff, P. G. (1992). *"Family Planning in Japanese Society"*. Princeton, NJ: Princeton University Press.

9. Trinh, t. n. l. (2002). *"Vietnamese traditional family values."* available from www.vietspring.org/values/tradionval.html.

10. Sun-Him, C. (1987*). "Introduction to Cambodian Culture. San Diego: SDSU Multicultural Resource Center"*.

11. Collins, E. F. And Bahar, E. (1995). *"Malu: Shame, Gender, Hierarchy, And Sexuality"*. Athens, Oh: Ohio University (Unpublished).

12. https://www.indyatour.com/india/culture/india-family-system.php

13. Tagiuri, R., & Davis, J. (1996). *"Bivalent Attributes of the Family Firm"*. Family Business Review, 9(2), 199–208. https://doi.org/10.1111/j.1741-6248.1996.00199.x

14. https://johndavis.com/family-resilience-in-the-time-ofcorona/?utm_source=rss&utm_medium=rss&utm_campaign=family-resilience-in-the-time-of-corona

Chapter 2

Family Values and Vision

Introduction

This chapter focuses on the role of values and vision building for the family, business and the members. Values are important features of family and culture building. Practice of Values will show, who you are and in some cultures from which family the member actually comes from. Moreover, the family business intentions, (most of the families) are to build a business for several generations and long lasting companies. The values, beliefs and ambitions of the families are the driving forces behind the culture of sustainability among family businesses. A study conducted by researchers from the IESE Business School, Spain came with the results that series of values that are characteristics of family business; generosity, humility, communication, service, quality, excellence, creativity and entrepreneurship. The largest family owned firms seem to have the three main characteristics; they emphasize a collective orientation; they have long term perspective and they have sense of stewardship. (Lucia, Remei and Josep, 2010)[1]. Long term perspective and stewardship are commonly found values among the family business groups. I therefore, through this chapter wanted to throw the light to the readers that identifying values and instilling within the family and subsequent generations will help the family businesses sustain their business and build institutions which will have longer life span and several generations will run the business.

Values

Values are important elements in one's life. Values are individual beliefs that motivate people to act one way or another. They serve as a guide for human behavior. Generally, people are predisposed to adopt the values that they are raised with. People also tend to believe that those values are "right" because they are the values of their family or particular culture.

Values denote the degree of importance of an action, with the aim of determining what actions are best for the situation and to maintain peace in life. Value systems (the collection of values one has is referred to as a value system) are proscriptive and prescriptive beliefs; they affect the ethical behavior of a person or are the basis of their intentional activities. People generally have two types of values; one is called Terminal and the other is called instrumental (Rokeach, 1973)[2]. These are also often known as primary values and secondary values. The primary values are stable for a long time in life and secondary values may change depending on one's progress and learning in life. For example, when you start your career, success is measured by status and money and that will be top priority. But after one has married, success measured based on the work-life balance will be of high value, meaning it is not only the money and status that matters, but how you manage the family as well.

For understanding more on the Instrumental and Terminal Values I produce the list of values produced by (Rokeach, 1973)[2].

Terminal Values	Instrumental Values
A comfortable life (a prosperous life)	Ambitious (hardworking)
An exciting life (a stimulating, active life)	Broadminded (open-minded)
A sense of accomplishment (lasting contribution)	Capable (competent, efficient)
A world of peace (free of war and conflict)	Cheerful (lighthearted, joyful)
A world of beauty (the beauty of nature and the arts)	Clean (neat, tidy)
Equality (brotherhood, equal opportunity for all)	Courageous (standing up for your beliefs)
Family security (taking care of loved ones)	Forgiving (willing to pardon)
Freedom (independence, free choice)	Helpful (working for the welfare of others)
Happiness (contentedness)	Honest (sincere, truthful)
Inner harmony (freedom from inner conflict)	Imaginative (daring, creative)
Mature love (sexual and spiritual intimacy)	Independent (self-reliant, self-sufficient)
National security (protection from attack)	Intellectual (intelligent, reflective)
Pleasure (an enjoyable, leisurely life)	Logical (consistent, rational)
Salvation (saved, eternal)	Loving (affectionate, tender)
Self-respect(self-esteem)	Obedient (dutiful, respectful)
Social recognition (respect, admiration)	Polite (courteous, well-mannered)
A true friend (close companionship)	Responsible (dependable, reliable)
Wisdom (a mature understanding of life)	Self-controlled (restrained, self-disciplined)

(Reproduced with permission from Sandra J Ball Rokeach)[2]

The values that a family practices and the way the children are raised are important aspects as they mature. Values are also learned from external sources: nation, society and the local community. Therefore, the children who grow up in different backgrounds will learn their specific values naturally.

The term "family values," though perhaps new to the reader, also has importance in the context of family businesses. What the family holds as values also naturally will be practiced in their business. The first generation of a family business always wants their own values practiced, progressing it for generation after generation. Therefore, the term has become a popular phrase in recent years in family business conversations. These family values define what is meaningful to your family—the beliefs and ideas that bind your family together. Different families around the world hold different values and beliefs.

Most family values may be classified as follows:

Moral Values

Moral values are the standards of good and evil, which govern an individual's behavior and choices. Individual's morals may get triggered from family, society and government, religion, or through self-learning. Moral values also guide "Right" and "Wrong" thinking, feelings and behaviour throughout one's life. Individuals tend to follow the moral values they have learned, and practice these continuously throughout their lives. Moral values also may change during one's life due to an intense experience or change of such moral teachings by spiritual organizations and sometimes from the change of a law.

We often read that choices are made in the decision-making processes of corporations that ensure maximum profits rather than considering the impact on other aspects in the organization, its workers, or the external environment. Businesses will also have demands from the markets to show profits and investors and stakeholders frequently trying to influence companies to cut their cost in all possible manners, at the expense of employee welfare. Research suggests that moral values are more prevalent in family than non-family firms (Sorenson, R. 2013)[3].

In theory, family businesses are well-positioned to resist such temptations. Because most family businesses are privately held, their owners are often shielded from the pressure of quarterly reports. Instead, they can make business decisions that might look irrational to the outside world — forgoing opportunities, investing in strategies that might not make any financial sense on paper — but that are consistent with their family's values and long-term goals. That means that family businesses built on a history of integrity, *should* be more immune to those temptations. For them, it's not just business, it's personal. (Loreto and Lachenauer, 2019)[4].

One of my clients, in the business of polymer packaging solutions, called Venbro Polymers at Erode, Tamilnadu in India, is very strongly driven by the family's moral values. Deriving inspiration and learning from the founder, they devote a great deal of time, investment and patience in employee performance. The result is very unique to their family business; well trained and competent employees, highly loyal to the organization and family, employment longevity with the organization, and more.

While talking about the moral values, for some people, an oral agreement is enough to keep the promise made in the absence of a formal contract. Another client that is in the retail sector, a popular brand in India called Cycle Brand pure *agarbathis* (incense sticks) belonging to NR Group is known for their commitment of payments to vendors or any service providers (including my services). The payment is made within the stipulated time period over the submission of the invoices. The value systems here is that the vendors shouldn't suffer due to delay or nonpayment. The practice is directly connected with the grandfather's (founder) experience, as he had a strong value for supporting his suppliers. His word was his bond. The erstwhile chairman of the group, Mr. Guru told me that he had witnessed from his father (founder) that sometimes the vendors never even had a signed contract, just a handshake agreement. The word is more important than any formal contract for the founder and that moral value is learned and practiced even after 50 years after the demise of the founder.

Another impressive example of family business and moral value is that of "Trust."A second-generation entrepreneur raised funds from a private source for his venture into construction projects. When he was struggling to pay off the money he had borrowed, his father insisted on selling off a property and clear the debts. The father had guided the son on, why trust among the financiers? It is very important to remain in business.

With all these examples, for family businesses, it is very important that they clearly define and reinforce their moral values for succeeding generations. The family must develop a system to ensure that when the next generation comes to the business, they have enough learning and knowledge of the moral values of the family. Moral values are needed to form a unique identity in the family business.

Personal Conduct and Social Behavior

Asian families are almost always relationship oriented, as we have seen in the first chapter. Strong relationships as one of the core values – the way one conducts one or oneself in a social setting, is noticed by the family members and by others. Asian cultures demand a high level of personal conduct such as respect for elders, empathy as a quality and more. These values guide the way in how we treat others and in how we stand up for those who need help within one's circles and society.

Defining what is good behavior, and setting up one's self as an example, always goes a long way in making these values and behaviours become intrinsic in our children. Good illustrations of social behaviours in many families include being respectful, good listeners, sharing, and showing and compassion to others, and caring for others' welfare. In our closest relationships, our values help shape our roles in life, relative to what it means to be a good husband, a good wife, a good parent, or a good sibling. Values give us our roadmaps for developing healthy relationships.

Our values shape the manner in which we conduct ourselves in personal interactions and as productive members of society. Showing respect for women, elders, and authority figures, treating people with kindness, and standing up for those who can't stand up for themselves are often key values for families. These values also can help teach children to keep their composure when things don't always go their way, instead fostering patience and resilience.

In order to help the younger generations, understand such demands from the family, effective family business consultants will identify these values through carrying out a systematic study of the family and the business. We make documentation of what is acceptable and what is not acceptable in the family and the family business. For example, value oriented dress codes, manners, and behaviours are thrust when one represents the family in social functions. Drug abuse, addictions to alcohol and tobacco, female harassment, are not accepted. The family "constitution" documents that I utilize describe the consequences for violations of the family/business values, even up to the loss of one's position in the business. Since personal conduct and social behaviour have significant impacts on the business and progress, it is essential that the elders of the family to instill the family values in the next generation, from early childhood onward.

Family Time

Family time is important. A healthy family and solid family relationships are important goals. Everyone in the family needs to ensure adequate time for others in the family. The time spent with the family is always valuable and is highly influential, leading to such as strong bondage, love, understanding, compassion and deep relationships among the family members. Family is an important shock absorber and spending quality time with family helps in coping with challenges, instills a feeling of security, inculcates family values, and fills kids with confidence and a moral compass, and much more.

Parents strive hard to earn money by working and being involved in the business. In the early part of their careers, parents may work and earn money for the family's comforts and security, but once the offspring arrive, the parent's focus must include the children's wellbeing. Asian families (and many others) have a deep cultural value of protecting and building wealth for the next generations. These families ensure the security of next generations by building assets. Finding time for the family and building wealth and assets are like the two sides of the same coin. It is challenging, of course, but it is strongly recommended to find time for the children, to share stories, hardships and successes, creating nice moments, inspiring, lessons on values and more. Few family businesses in India have emphasized the value of family time in their family practices and family constitutions. The Murugappa Group from Chennai and GMR Group in Bangalore are the good examples to quote.

The following paragraphs are written with more emphasis on family time as a value. As one family may value profit as the most important value, another family may have charity as the most important value. It is not possible to determine what the best values are for everyone, as it is impossible to impose values upon business families from outside. Hence, the objective of reinforcing family time as a value may be important to each family.

The concept of "family" has changed over the years, as explained above. There are various forms of families and different styles of parenting. However, one thing remains certain; whatever the term "family" may mean to you, it is of utmost importance and influence in your children's lives. HOW a parent BEHAVES is more influential on the children than how that same parent TELLS the children to behave.

The family in which your child grows up has a big influence on how he or she deals with relationships, copes with situations, and learns about living life. The best outcomes are only possible if you as a parent behave using the values you wish the children to adopt. And for this to happen, you need to block family time in your schedule. Family time is also important because if children don't get the enough attention, they are more likely to involve in activities that will get them into trouble.

Parents at home who have no or other home bound work may think that they are somehow "better" than other parents, who are away from home for most of the time. This is a misconception.

In my personal experience with various family businesses, the issue of time spent with their children is often "how *much* time they spend" rather than how much *undistracted* time and quality attention is given to the child. We often think of *quantity* of time when it comes to the time we spend with our kids, whereas it is the *quality* of the time that we need to devote to family and children. Some Indian business families have a family "rule" that everyone is assembled at the dinner table every day at a specified time. They also organize Sunday brunch meetings with all the family members or fortnightly excursions with kids. Also, quarterly outings for a few days and annual international travels also are planned. However, with this planning, one important aspect is how much devoted attention and personal conversation you offer to them. Your children care less about the hours you spend with them than how you spend those hours with them.

As your children get older and become teenagers, it becomes more challenging to spend good quality family time with them. It is mainly because life keeps you busy and your children reach a stage where they will start chasing their own interests, dreams, goals, education and friends.

According to various studies, healthy families make family time for talking and listening, accepting differences, showing affection and encouragement, sharing chores and decision making, keeping in touch, and making time for each other.

In Indian families, the grandparents play a vital role in fulfilling the need for attention to the children. Since the grandparents have the direct experiences of their own children, how their children moved on in their lives, the struggles and challenges they faced and, sharing those experiences with the grandchildren is a high source of inspiration. It is important to share the value practices of the parents in both personal life and business life. The values demonstrated by decision making, relationships, and charity decisions by the parents will give enhanced understanding to the children.

Important Life Lessons

In the present world, learning comes from different directions, but knowing and learning the right lessons really matters. Instead of allowing children to waste time, undergo pain, struggles and constraints, is it possible for the parent to transfer the important learning that is needed? The current generation knows what they want in life, and what they want to learn. My son who is currently studying Computer Science Engineering, in a college is always busy and engaged with busy project schedules. We were concerned as parents about his eating and sleeping habits. When we were together at the dinner table, I would express my concern and his reply would be "wait for some time until I finish the projects." We used to keep quiet. In a month's time he came and declared that he had been selected for the University Innovation Fellowship offered by Stanford University, in the USA. We are proud parents today. Though this story looks impressive, it is important to have family time for discussions. During these family times we can put forth challenges in the family and business or situations in front of them, and then talk about them with children, seek their opinion, and discuss the matter. Share your views and how you have solved, or proposed to solve, problems so that they know different ways of looking at the issues and help them learn from the experiences of other family members. This would help them understand a wider range of situations of life in a more effective way.

Apart from learning, we also use family time for showing affection to each other, giving hugs, holding hands, being thoughtful and kind, and instilling a sense of security in life. According to Carl Pickhardt (2012)[5], teenagers who remember being recognized, praised, and hugged within the family are likely to do better at school than those who don't have this experience. Hence, make an effort to think about the positive qualities in each person and tell your child what goodness you have noticed, besides teaching them these values.

Family Identities, Rituals and Practices

Daily rituals, or the little things that you do regularly and on special occasions, help building a sense of belonging, contentedness, and inner security within the family. Daily rituals like the way you greet each other, or say goodbye, what you do at mealtimes or bedtimes, can all be something to share within your family time.

Families benefit from coming together to celebrate occasions like birthdays, anniversaries, or festivals like Chinese New Year, Christmas, etc., where they learn the traditions associated with these times.

Help Them to Accept Differences in the Family

Diversity is strength in today's economy. Learning to accept, understand and embrace diversity within the family and outside will help the next generations to successfully run the business. Diversity in terms of gender, religion, race and nationality is a norm in present organizations. Therefore, families that share and extend their understanding about the benefits of having a diverse workforce gains importance in the future leadership of the family business. This learning can occur only when the children in the family are taught and given opportunities to learn the differences within the family. It is essential to appreciate, encourage, and value the differences in each family member, knowing that everyone is special in their own way. Allow each family member to be excited about their personal interests and show respect and tolerance towards them. This will help in promoting the idea of acceptance of diversity in family, business, and society at large.

The importance of family and why you should spend quality time with family is no longer questioned. Now you know it helps create a sense of belonging, where you can share ideas, values, and beliefs. You will build a stronger family unit by spending more time together, and your family will stick together through rough times, besides enjoying the fun times together.

Show loyalty to your family, stick up for each other so that each person feels confident in the family's support and pulls together to form a combined line-up to find solutions. Children grow up and are gone elsewhere before you realize it, so don't waste the time you have now, and spend it with your family. Remember, that strong families are able to withstand setbacks and crisis with the positive attitude, shared values, and beliefs that help them cope with challenges.

Building Vision for the Family and the Business

A vision is a statement of a desired or ideal outcome. Building a vision is a way of getting clarity on what a person or business wants to attain. The destination is identified and targeted before the journey begins. Vision provides a road map along with expected challenges and opportunities. It also includes one's desires, dreams and goals. Hence, building a vision becomes an essential exercise at any level, say individual, family and enterprise.

Building a Vision Helps in Two Ways

First, vision gives propulsion towards the destination you desire. It inspires you and generates an abundance of energy. Vision guides and makes your journey a purposeful one; and it opens up the deepest motivations or passions. Making the connection between the innermost motivation and the journey towards the destination will make one unstoppable. You may never actually reach your vision, but its existence will pull you forward. When progress slows, you can reenergize the forward pulling drive by creating a new, even bigger vision.

Second, it provides guidance in a world of choices. It enables you to focus on what to do (and not do) to reach those achievements five or ten years or more in the future. When you are clear about your vision and goals, it is easier to say "yes" wholeheartedly or say "no" with an acceptable reason and without fear of rejection. To quote an example, one of the well-known business groups in India has multiple sugar mills at different locations. Their sugar production gives molasses as a by-product of the processes. Molasses is the raw material for alcohol production and this group could have entered the distillery business with ease and made good profits. But the founder was not willing to enter that business, as he had a vision for himself and the group of companies, so that they will never take part in any business that negatively impacts people and society. He vehemently refused to enter in the liquor distillery business despite had an opportunity to make more profits. The vision helped the group chairman to make the decision.

Simon Sinek mentions in his *TEDx Talk*, (September 2009) (https://www.youtube.com/watch?v=u4ZoJKF_VuA) and in his book, *Start with Why*, that every individual or company needs to know their "why" to get the remainder (the "what" and the "how") correct and sorted out. According to Sinek, if you know the "Why," you will easily figure out the "What" and the "How" later. Enlarge and concentrate on the biggest, long-term version of your vision.

In order to build your vision and develop plans based on that vision, consider Google's corporate vision[6] as a good example. It is: "***To provide access to the world's information in one click.***" The nature of Google's business is a direct manifestation of this vision statement. For example, Google's most popular product is its search engine service. This product enables people to easily access information from around the world. Also, the statement is brief and is easy to understand and remember; and to communicate to others.

The pointers discussed in the following paragraph can directly be compared with Google Vision statement.

When we help family business organizations build their own visions, we generally work on the following points to ensure that a stimulating and appropriate vision statement is created.

Unambiguous: The vision statement should be straight-forward and self-explanatory.

Simple: Write it directly and succinctly so that it is quick and easy to grasp and can be easily repeated by any employee at any given time.

Specific: Narrow – not too broad.

Bold: Is it brave and big enough? Stretch yourself rather than staying inside the status quo.

Aligned: Your vision, and the pathway towards it, should be aligned. Most importantly, they should have internal integrity. For instance, a company that tries to change the world positively also needs to have processes and rules that are positive on the inside.

Inspiring: Write your vision in an inspirational manner. Think of a sci-fi movie trailer that pulls millions into the cinema; your vision should have a similar captivating pull to it.

Engaging: Creating your vision is like building a house: you might not know how to build the house yourself, but you have ideas and images in your mind that you pass onto an architect who helps you create sketches and plans from which to construct and achieve the final product, together.

Personal Vision

Developing a personal vision can guide the individual to take the journey of life towards a desired destination in both personal and professional success. Your vision for your life helps you to set goals and make decisions every day. When creating your personal vision, reflect from different perspectives and think of what you desire to have, to be, to give and to do. Ideally, if there were no limits or constraints, what would you contribute to this world, or help your inner circle, your community or even all the people on this planet to accomplish? Thinking of this often reveals or clarifies your real purpose in life.

Organizational Vision

An organizational vision is the centerpiece and foundation of all corporate strategies and goal setting. The vision functions as the "*north star*," it points to the everyday work of employees as a contribution towards the ultimate long-term accomplishment. Overall, a good vision is something you hear once and then never forget. Creating a stretch beyond what you think is possible in the real world is important. When the "pull" of the vision weakens as you get close to accomplishing it, revise the vision to a great new healthy "pull."

Family Vision

Like building personal and organization vision, it is also helpful if families also build their own vision. Generally, the vision comes from the founder of the business from the family and guides the family members on a set of values, principles and ethics. Though frequently analyzed, the vision from the founder is unwritten, nor formally stated; rather it is seen as an action and shared in informal sharing. Later it becomes a habit and ritual within the company. Many family businesses run charity foundations, taking the cue from the founder's practice of supporting the needy and the society. However, when the family moves to the second and third generations in the family businesses, I recommend the vision building for the families as an important exercise as it will help the families to move forward with clarity and value practice. Making it formal and having a document make the family more concrete in their direction. Therefore, it is highly recommended to develop a vision for the family. The vision is drafted by collecting each member's desires and dreams including the values they believe in. Usually group process approaches are used for such purposes in a workshop setting. All the members of the family participate in these workshops and contribute their views and ideas in building a vision for the family. After it is given approval by everyone, the vision statement is written and communicated to all the stakeholders within the family and outside family.

Once the family vision is approved and communicated to all the stakeholders, it becomes a shared vision of the family. Lack of a shared vision is one of the most significant threats to the sustainability of a family business through multiple generations of family ownership. A vision needs to be created, and then updated as necessary. Professor Steve Miller's research (as quoted by *Cooper Biersach (BA '91, MBA/ JD '96)* https://www.kenan-flagler.unc.edu/news/6-tips-for-creating-a-shared-vision-for-your-family-business/website)*has found that in addition to being a critical success factor, having a shared vision is strongly predictive of the presence of effective next-generation family business leaders.

If shared vision is so critical to family business continuity, how does a business-owning family create it? Miller's research demonstrates that open and transparent communication in the family is one of the keys, as it strongly predicted the presence of a shared vision for the business. On the other hand, a previous generation that exercises unquestioned authority and makes all the rules was even more strongly predictive of the lack of a shared vision. That kind of autocratic leadership style can shut down the open communication that is so necessary to the development of a shared vision for the future of the family firm.

Developing a vision and strategy: Steve Miller (2014)[8] suggests beginning conversations with key family leaders about their long-term desires and goals for the company. Ask everyone *why* you are in this business together.

1. Think about your company's current strategy and how it might need to change to reflect growth or changes in the industry over the next 10-15 years. Talk to the current leader of your family firm to get his/her perspective.

2. Imagine a future for your business in which all things are possible.

3. Traditional business education teaches us to focus on solving problems. While problem-solving is an important skill, creating an inspiring vision for your family enterprise requires suspending a focus on constraints — at least temporarily. Ask "what would be ideal" rather than "what would be possible."

4. Create your shared vision and subsequent strategy grounded in an understanding of market dynamics. Researching and analyzing market data can be an outstanding assignment for developing next-generation leaders.

5. Identify and develop plans for closing performance gaps. While envisioning a new future for the family firm and developing strategies to capitalize on market opportunities is exciting and motivating, it's important to close performance gaps in the execution of your current strategies first. You might be tempted to try to correct a performance problem by introducing a new product or service, employing a new strategy or even creating a new business, when the real issue is poor execution of your current strategy.

6. Keep in mind to communicate on a regular basis with the family owners, including those who are not active in the management of the business. The goal is to create commitment to your shared vision of the family firm, and that requires input from

ALL major stakeholders. Owners may modify their goals once the firm's management has helped them understand what it will take to achieve them. The process tends to be an illustrative one, with plenty of back and forth communication among the owners and management.

Summary

In this chapter the importance of values for family business for sustaining the business for long term is being discussed. Values play a major role in building culture and institutions. Understanding of instrumental and terminal values, moral values and personal conduct & behaviors are the keys to successful transition from generation to generation in order to hold on to the founder's values and make it as a successful business and organization. Vision building on the other hand offers a way in which the family would travel in consensus with all family members to achieve its primary goals in terms of business and family. The six steps for vision building and strategy by Steve Miller explains how the process of building vision can be achieved.

References

1. Ceja, Lucia and Agulles, Remei and Tàpies, Josep (2010), "*The Importance of Values in Family-Owned Firms*", IESE Business School Working Paper No. 875,. SSRN: https://ssrn.com/abstract=1701642 or http://dx.doi.org/10.2139/ssrn.1701642

2. Rokeach (1973) "*The Nature of Human Value*s, The Free Press Copy Right renewedat 2001, by Samdara J Ball-Rokeach.

3. Sorenson, R. (2013*), " How moral and social values become bedded in family firms*", Journal of Management Spirituality and Religion, (10) (2), pp. 116-137

4. Nick Di Loreto, and Rob Lachenauer (2019), "5 *Signs That Your Family Business Might Have an Ethics Problem*",

5. Carl Pickhardt (2012), https://www.psychologytoday.com/us/blog/surviving-your-childs-adolescence/201201/adolescence-and-the-development-habits

6. http://panmore.com/google-vision-statement-mission-statement

7. *Cooper Biersach (BA '91, MBA/JD '96), co-founder and director of the Family Enterprise Centerasmentioned in the website* http://familyenterprise.unc.edu/

8. Stephen P. Miller (2014), "*Next-generation leadership development in family businesses: the critical roles of shared vision and family climate*", Frontiers in Psychology.

Chapter 3

The Reciprocity of Love, Gratitude and the Affirmative Benefits to the Family

Introduction

I have a reason for including this chapter in the book. I see many family businesses that do extremely good business but fail miserably on the family front. All family businesses confront many challenges and conflicts in order to be united and stay together in business. I have consulted with a family which is in the tier distribution and retreading business. There were three brothers and their father was the founder of the business. The business was doing very well, but the brothers were having issues among themselves. All the brothers were trained absolutely in this business and were having enough inputs about it. Finally, they have decided to split, and part within themselves and leave what is so far perceived to be a family business.

After the split, each one of them opened alternative tire distribution and retreading show rooms in the same city, and they fiercely battled to pick up customers. The result was obvious: the family and the business together collapsed. The learning is clear: business families need to learn, inculcate, and promote the qualities of love, reciprocity, and gratitude. The equity among them should pick up in time and spirit so that it can contribute the business in different skills rather than dissimilar interests. This chapter deals with the necessity of bonding and being together closely as a family, how mutually respect and share everything together, still maintaining the boundaries and spaces for each individual and their families. It takes years to learn and understand to express gratitude for what the founder's family is offering and how the next generations respect what they have inherited, which are built over the years.

Reciprocity

"Reciprocity refers to the exchanging of resources between people," says Kelly Campbell, a professor of psychology at California State University, San Bernardino. Campbell, while explaining reciprocity, she shares some basic examples of this concept, like lending money (financial capital) or providing a service (Human Capital), which can be repaid in a length of time that corresponds to the relationship's intimacy level. I have 3 hectares (7 acres) of land; I usually lease it out due to not having enough time to take care of the property. The lease is prearranged generally to a nuclear family. I found, as a routine the cousins of the family come to help with the work, such as preparing the soil, sowing seeds, adding manure and fertilizers, irrigating, harvesting, and making storage. In turn, this family pitches in whenever there is a need for extra manpower to support the cousins. Thereby, they minimize the expenses by reciprocating with labour. Also, loaning money with no interest is a common practice; but with a strict pay back date. I have always admired this quality in them of supporting each other's professions and living.

This can be a classical example of reciprocity. We all do this in several ways. We exchange or share our resources when others are in need. Will that be the same in families which are involved in large businesses? There are mixed experiences. Many families in business as family business together support their members very well, remain united and reciprocate with lots of love, gratitude and wealth. Also, there are families that fail family business as the one family which was in the tire (layer on the wheel) business shown in the earlier paragraph.

Reciprocity gets more interesting—and more challenging—when you consider its nuances. A more intimate relationship tends to be full of understanding, but that's not something one should take it for granted.

"Within relationships, it is important that reciprocity is balanced," Campbell adds. "If one person is doing all of the giving, and the other is doing all of the receiving, then the relationship is lopsided and at risk for dissatisfaction, infidelity, or dissolution." Cited in Kelly Dawson's (2020)[1] article in the website. In order to build a healthy relationship, it's always good to know where you stand in the realm of reciprocity, and where you need to improve.

Relationship Matters

Every relationship is important. History has proven that we all live in unison, share the resources together and the tendencies of fraternity, mother's love and benevolence towards others too. Being in a social relationship, each one of us looks for a closeness and bonding with someone. The first bonding comes between the mother and children and gets expanded over a time. But the bonding between mother and child is special and unconditional; moreover it is innate and natural. However, every other relationship requires effort, investment of time, the expression of love, and too often these relationships become conditional in nature. I'll give you love only if you do something which is needed or memorable for me. These relationships are based on a give and take nature too. Love and romance related relationships may be exceptional in certain cases. Marriage relationships are another example: two adults decide to come together and love each other by way of getting married, as described in Asian cultures, most of the time the parents alone search and find the groom or bride for the marriage. In such circumstances, building relationships are quite challenging because the married partners are completely strangers that any personal dynamism to take off, and love to culminate, it will catch more time in between. That is a period which is more stressful and sometimes would even lead to bitter experiences. "Marriage relationships plummet a lot" as shared by one of my friends who is in family therapy practice. "Divorce cases are increasing in India as quoted by a news paper Deccan Herald[2]. But there is light always at the end of the tunnel that there are many ways one can improve familial relationships and live positively[2].

Edgar Schein (2013)[3] recommends, the "Humble Inquiry" for building positive relationships and better organizations. He writes in his book *Humble Inquiry (2013)* that the way to build a positive relationship is not by telling people what to do, rather asking people gently for agreement to act in a certain way. He argues that this is an art.

According to Schein, *telling* puts the other person down. This often means that one is assuming that the other person does not know what is needed, and therefore, I must tell him. When this kind of communication happens, the other person gets impatient at a minimum and, at maximum, gets offended or will be annoyed. However, *asking* temporarily empowers the other person in the conversation and momentarily makes the asking person vulnerable. It's an investment one makes to build the relationship. A conversation that leads to a relationship has to be equitable, inviting, and balanced.

Campbell suggests that "reciprocity" is one of the ways to build a strong relationship.

When we think of a relationship, we probably think of a romantic relationship that requires building through regular instances of reciprocity. However, any relationship that you have in your life— from parents to siblings to friends to co-workers—can benefit from reciprocity. And since this word is all about acknowledging someone's kindness toward you, it can even be something that you practice with acquaintances and deserving strangers.

"Although it sounds a bit cold, people can start to keep tabs on how much they are giving and receiving," Campbell says. "Luckily, the amount you give is largely under your control." (Kelly, 2020)

"Conversely, if people aren't giving enough, you can let them know your feelings, and allow them the time to make adjustments," she continues. "If you've communicated your needs and nothing changes, it may be time to sever those unhealthy relationships." (Kelly, 2020).

Campbell notes that satisfaction and commitment grow over time in a relationship that has balanced reciprocity. In most cases, it comes down to the three basics of open communication, clear expectations, and mutual respect. "The healthiest relationships are the ones in which both partners are fulfilling each other's needs on a regular basis" she says (Kelly, 2020). She also recommends practicing reciprocity in five types of relationships: Family, friends, siblings, co-workers, and strangers. These five are always important in many ways, as we are always in need of them. Strangers may be exceptional in this case.

I come from a large family born with six elder sisters and grew up in a neighbourhood, which was very friendly and supportive in many ways. Since I was an only son to my mother and the only brother to my six sisters, I was always being pampered. My sisters are wonderful women and they are too elderly to me. This has made me grow among not just one mother but many as they showered me with much love and sympathy; it is just like natural for women too, isn't it? This environment made me feel secure and developed an expectation that everyone around me is there only to give. I started complaining when I was not given what I expected others to give to me. It took such a long time to learn that the world is not centred on me! Such a one was my immaturity that was affecting every one of my relationships. The insight came to me when I attended a personal development workshop. The insight helped me to change and I learned to look outward more, and I realized that I also needed to give back. When I started practicing this, it is not at all easy, as old habits die hard (I had to be conscious continuously and consistently), the wonders started happening in my relationships. One of my friends, who continuously guided me in this direction, was always demanding the quality of time, which I always got whenever I needed. The moment I realized this and started responding positively, the relationship improved significantly. Perhaps the turning point in my evolution as a person was the day; I realized that I needed to give something in return to those who helped me. I now believe that expecting others to help me, out of pure benevolence, is a sign of both immaturity and foolhardiness.

Reciprocity also means "giving back" to the people who are giving positive things to you. As I learned, this hard lesson, my life and relationships improved dramatically.

Let us now look at how this will be helpful in family business landscapes.

The Value of Love

But let there be spaces in your togetherness and let the winds of the heavens dance between you. Love one another but make not a bond of love: let it rather be a moving sea between the shores of your souls.

– Khalil Gibran, 'The Prophet'.

I believe all of us were given the tremendous blessings of being able to love one another and to be loved. It's important to recognize that these are two different things. The act of loving someone else is self-giving. It is not just a thought — it is an action we take purely with the selfless, altruistic intention of providing benefit for someone else.

Accepting love from another requires that we become conscious of what love is and how do we perceive it? And inculcate it in us, as a sensibility. It is taking into an awareness of the fact of being loved. Then, we willingly allow ourselves to be loved and let the kindness, beauty and goodness of that beyond word emotion purifies us ever and ever. The 'cup must be empty' is a Zen saying. Keep your mind emptied, with no rag in it, so that untarnished love can fill in entirely.

Building relationships is imperative; that we are very much limited to fulfill that exclusively by ourselves is a challenge. In order to build the relationships, one has to move from the spotlight on oneself and focus the one who receives it. If we compassionately listen to another person with whom you want to build a relationship, it does wonders as he/she understands the value of the relationship. I said earlier that loving is self-giving. One of the ways to do this is to be genuinely curious and engaged in conversations with others. You learn more about the other individual and you may get valuable new information that will benefit you as well. By expressing concern and empathy on others, you gain an admiration out of that relationship. That someone will then want to learn more about you and what your concerns are about.

The problem is the world does not automatically work this way. It may be as simple as citing the law of supply and demand, but it goes even further than this through the impulses and emotions of the human psyche. Inherently, we are made up of and created by nature that love should be the back force of all our deeds and acts which ultimately makes as a unique life form on earth. Though we are called social animals we are not animals in a true sense. We have certain inherent qualities in us; tender emotions, generosity, altruism and kind acts of virtue that simultaneously make the lives of others better.

Considering the above background, within families, members must practice reciprocity of love, gratitude and wealth. Usually in Asian cultures, families are intergenerational. Sometimes there will be three generations living in the same home and also as joint families. In such circumstances, there are always lots of "giving and taking" required. The elder generations take care of the grandchildren to facilitate their children to focus on their work and business, and in reciprocity the grandchildren do provide great benefit to the grandparents. I see this in many families. However, in joint families, it becomes more complex, as there will be more members of the same generation living together, say brothers and their wives. As we understand, many Asian families have the practice of the bride coming and living in the husband's home and she has the onus of running a family from cooking to carry on other household chores and raising the children.

Reciprocity among the Multi Generations

In the article written by Timothy and Ellie (1999)[4], when individuals live longer, their opportunities for multiple generational contact increases. For example, today there is a 60 percent chance that a 60-year-old female will have a living parent (Watkins, Menken, & Bongaarts, 1987)[5], and it is likely that she is also a grandparent (Robertson, 1996)[6]. These intergenerational relationships are characterized by respect, responsibility, reciprocity, and resiliency. Regardless of the generation (older, middle, and younger) of focus, respect, responsibility, reciprocity, and resiliency are evident within the relationships these characteristics are relevant to individuals who work with older people and their families. These characteristics can be used as foundations on which to further strengthen intergenerational bonds.

Ramakrishna, the greatest Bengali saint once instructed his disciple who is tirelessly on a practice of '*hatha yoga*', a physical exercise invented by ancient saints of India, to first take care of his mother and then come to his ashram to practice yoga. So the family responsibility comes first. When families themselves do business then the business will become a responsibility of a whole family

In all the lives of us normal individual intergenerational relationships are characterized by reciprocity. While younger generations support older relatives, older relatives are assisting younger persons. In short, intergenerational relationships in the later years are a boulevard with a two-way lane. The classic example that many people readily observe is the childcare provided by many grandparents, and the emotional support adult children and grandchildren render their grandparents. (Timothy and Elly, 1999)[4].

However, the reciprocity is a connecting mechanism between the generations. practicing reciprocity among the same generation is found to be a real challenge in my personal experience. In joint families, when the wives of the brothers of the family live in the same home or even in different homes, the stretch of the relationship is always put on a test due to the power of who has more say in family affairs. As the family practice goes in most of the Asian families, the eldest son and his wife have more say on many of the affairs of the family, and this often is not very well accepted among the other ladies in the home. Everyone aspires to be part of the decision making course and expects to at least be part of the consensus process. This is where we, as family business consultants, recommend the *family council* as a solution. When there is a conflict within the family, it starts reflecting in many other forums including the family council. Family council is probably a platform where the family members at least work on the following areas to make a smooth transition into family and business success.

Most Family Councils seek to address the important matters impacting their business family, including:

- Aligning multiple family members for a single voice of the family,
- Preparing for and facilitating generational transition, including family, communication and education on legal matters and estate planning,
- Communication and conflict resolution processes for the challenges that naturally arise out of the family to the business,
- Family member development and education for the next generations,
- Creating collective purpose, goals, vision, mission and values
- Philanthropic Initiatives – Running Family Foundations

We will learn more about the family council and its importance in the next chapters because we may carefully work on how a business is not just an individual entity but also bears social responsibility.

Gratitude

Gratitude is a word that shows the quality of being thankful; readiness to show appreciation for and to return kindness-- as per the oxford dictionary. However, the word Gratitude is just not a word. As found from the article written by Courtney E. Ackerman, (Psychology today, 29.04.2020, gratitude is regarded as either a trait (dispositional) or state (of being) [7]. As a trait, an individual practices gratitude as part of their daily life (McCullough, Emmons, & Tsang, 2002)[8] and it would be considered a characteristic strength, to possess gratitude. As a trait, gratitude can be developed with practice and awareness (Peterson, & Seligman, 2004)[9].

When a person experiences the rich emotion from someone expressing gratitude for them, it is referred to as a state (Watkins, Van Gelder, & Frias, 2009)[10]. Gratitude is both: a trait and a state. The state of being grateful is a pleasant experience studied by philosophers of ancient times.

Thesaurus gives equal words for the word gratitude as follows: acknowledgment, appreciative, grace, gracefulness, gratefulness, praise, recognition, requital, responsiveness and thankfulness. If we are using any of these words in conversation with others or act, say, recognizing, appreciating someone, then we are expressing the gratitude to the person. Practicing gratitude is an important quality in any human life.

Many of us express gratitude by saying "thank you" to someone who has helped us or given us a gift. From a scientific perspective, however, gratitude is not just an action: it is also a positive emotion that serves a biological purpose.

Positive psychology defines gratitude in a way where scientists can measure its effects, and thus argue that gratitude is more than a feeling of being thankful: it is a deeper appreciation for someone (or something) that produces longer lasting positivity.

Modern Psychological Perspectives on Gratitude

Positive psychology has expanded research on the importance of gratitude, largely led by researcher Robert Emmons. Emmons has authored several papers on the psychology of gratitude, showing that being more grateful can lead to increased levels of well-being (Emmons & Crumpler, 2000)[11]. Some of Emmons's works have also dealt specifically with gratitude in a religious setting, highlighting how feeling grateful towards a higher power may lead to increased physical health (Krause et al., 2013)[12].

Building Relationship through Gratitude:

Having explained about gratitude and its positive impact on the self and others, members within the family may benefit immensely by expressing gratitude among themselves. I have used the power of gratitude in many of my workshops with family business clients. I hand over a set of "post it" hand bills before the start of the workshops and ask the family members to find and write three reasons for having appreciative deeds amongst each others. I request them to hand it over to each others; as and when they finish the exercise, sometimes participants hand over the *post it* sheets towards the end of the workshop. Later, they would express that they actually had complaints or conflicts with the other individuals and would want to share that in the workshop. But this exercise made them think that there are better things to look at positively and would start writing the positive reasons to appreciate them, in other words express their gratitude. That is the power of practicing positive psychology or expressing gratitude to other people. I strongly advocate that family assemblies and family council meetings begin with the expression of gratitude to each other. Also, in general, people learn to express the thankfulness and gratitude to others within the family. Expression of gratitude is way of building a positive relationship.

I have taken four findings for the benefit of family business stakeholders to know, from the nine psychological findings quoted, related to the study of gratitude cited in the article written by Courtney E. Ackerman, (Psychology today, 2020):

1. Enhanced Well-being

Expressing your thanks can improve your overall sense of well-being. Grateful people are more agreeable, more open, and less neurotic (McCullough et al., 2002; McCullough, Tsang, & Emmons, 2004; (Wood, Maltby, Gillett, Linley, & Joseph, 2008)[13]

2. Deeper Relationships

Gratitude is also a powerful tool for strengthening interpersonal relationships. People who express their gratitude for each other tend to be more willing to forgive others and less narcissistic (DeShea, 2003[14]; Farwell & Wohlwend-Lloyd, 1998)[15].

Giving thanks to those who have helped you strengthens your relationships and promotes relationship formation and maintenance, as well as relationship connection and satisfaction (Aloge et al., 2008)[16]

3. Improved Optimism

Emmons and McCullough (2003)[17] in their study of exploring the impact of practicing gratitude, found that after 10 weeks, that people who focused on gratitude showed more optimism in many areas of their lives, including health and exercise. When people are optimistic about their well-being and health, they may be more likely to act in ways that support a healthy lifestyle.

4. Increased Happiness

Toepfer, Cichy, and Peters (2011)[18] conducted a study asking people to write and deliver a letter to someone for whom they were grateful. After the task, their happiness levels and life satisfaction were dramatically effected—even weeks later.

It will be interesting to see what is in store for future psychological investigations into gratitude.

The Positive Impact of Reciprocity and Gratitude in Relationships

Practicing reciprocity has many positive impacts on the relationships. It helps people to feel being recognized for those conducts they have done to others. The person who reciprocates also feels good about receiving a help. The "good feeling" which is created by the giver and the person who reciprocates feel upbeat about each other. I use this reciprocity as a tool in family business meetings. It works powerfully. Reciprocity practice promotes the positive aspects in relationships is supported by development psychologists Hartup and Stevens, (1997)[19] stating that throughout the life span reciprocity and mutuality is central features of friendships. Buunk and Wilmar (2011)[20] in their evolutionary analysis of reciprocal altruism, state that humans have developed innate mechanisms to expect reciprocity in interpersonal relationships and that a lack of reciprocity is accompanied by negative effect.

Expression of Gratitude on the other hand, has many positives associated in relationships as stated by several studies, which I quote some of them below. Gratitude may function to promote relationship formation and maintenance (Algoe et al., 2008)[16]. Perceived responsiveness is an appraisal that is associated with feeling understood, valued, and cared for by another individual (Reis et al., 2004)[21].Gratitude was uniquely associated with a reappraisal of the benefactor's positive qualities and promoted relationship-enhancing motivations toward the benefactor (Algoe & Haidt, 2008)[16].

I have quoted some of the research studies to make the readers to believe that practicing reciprocity and gratitude will result in positive impacts in relationships. Especially, in family business practices if the family members learn and start practicing these good aspects will result in lots of harmony and the feeling of togetherness.

Summary

The inclusion of this chapter or the topic has a background. In my review of literature survey in family business, I wasn't able to come across many studies that speak about the importance of reciprocity or gratitude. Therefore I decided to include such a topic for the benefit of the readers of this book, emphasizing the importance of reciprocity and gratitude, which in turn will help them to build good relationships among the family members and also extend to the other circles of relatives and friends.

References

1. Kelly Dawson: (2020) https://www.mydomaine.com/reciprocity-in-relationships

2. https://www.deccanherald.com/metrolife/metrolife-on-the-move/divorce-on-the-rise-among-the-rich-and-educated-806269.html

3. Edgar H. Schein (2013), *Humble Inquiry, The Gentle Art of Asking Instead of Telling* by Published by Berrett-Koehler Publishers.

4. Timothy H. Brubaker and Ellie Brubaker (1999), *The Four Rs of Intergenerational Relationships: Implications for Practice*, Michigan Family Review, Volume 04, Issue 1, Summer, pp. 5-15.

5. Watkins, S. C., Menken, J.A., & Bongaarts, J. (1987). *Demographic foundations of family change. American Sociological Review, 52*, 346-358.

6. Robertson, J. (1996). *Grand parenting in an era of rapid change*. In R. Blieszner & V. H. Bedford (Eds.) *Aging and the family* (pp.243-260). Westport, CT: Praeger.

7. Courtney Ackerman (2020) https://positivepsychology.com/gratitude-appreciation/

8. McCullough, M. E., Emmons, R. A., & Tsang, J.-A. (2002). *The grateful disposition: A conceptual and empirical topography. Journal of Personality and Social Psychology, 82*(1), 112–127. https://doi.org/10.1037/0022-3514.82.1.112

9. Park, N., Peterson, C., & Seligman, M. E. P. (2004). Strengths of character and well-being. *Journal of Social and Clinical Psychology, 23*(5), 603–619. https://doi.org/10.1521/jscp.23.5.603.50748

10. Watkins, Philip & Gelder, M. & Frias, A. (2012). *Furthering the Science of Gratitude*. Oxford handbook of positive psychology. 437-445. 10.1093/oxfordhb/9780195187243.013.0041

11. Emmons, Robert & Crumpler, Cheryl. (2000). *Gratitude as a Human Strength: Appraising the Evidence*. Journal of Social and Clinical Psychology. 19. 56-69. 10.1521/jscp.2000.19.1.56

12. Krause, Neal & Hayward, R. (2013). *Humility, Compassion, and Gratitude to God: Assessing the Relationships Among Key Religious Virtues*. 10.1037/rel0000028

13. Wood, Alex & Maltby, John & Stewart, Neil & Linley, P. & Joseph, Stephen. (2008). *A Social-Cognitive Model of Trait and State Levels of Gratitude.* Emotion (Washington, D.C.). 8. 281-90. 10.1037/1528-3542.8.2.281.

14. DeShea, Lise. (2016). *LiseDeShea does not recommend her scenario-based scale on willingness to forgive.*

15. Farwell, Lisa & Wohlwend-Lloyd, R. (1998). *Narcissistic Processes: Optimistic Expectations, Favorable Self-Evaluations, and Self-Enhancing Attributions.* Journal of personality. 66. 65-83. 10.1111/1467-6494. t01-2-00003.

16. Sara B Algoe, Jonathan Haidt, Shelly L Gable (2008), *Beyond reciprocity: gratitude and relationships in everyday life.* Emotion, Volume (83), (425-9).

17. Robert A. Emmons and Michael E. McCullough (2003) *"Counting Blessings Versus Burdens: An Experimental Investigation of Gratitude and Subjective Well-Being in Daily Life"* Journal of Personality and Social Psychology, Vol. 84, No. 2, 377–389

18. Toepfer, Steven &Cichy, Kelly & Peters, Patti. (2012*). Letters of Gratitude: Further Evidence for Author Benefits.* Journal of Happiness Studies. 13. 187-201. 10.1007/s10902-011-9257-7.

19. Hartup Willard and Stevens N, (1997) *Friendship and Adaptation in the Life Course,* Psychological Bulletin, (355-377).

20. Buunk B P and Schaufeli Wilmar, (2011) *Reciprocity in Interpersonal Relationships: An Evolutionary Perspective on Its Importance for Health and Well-being,* Journal of European Review of Social Psychology.

21. Reis HT, Clark MS, Holmes JG. (2004) *Perceived partner responsiveness as an organizing construct in the study of intimacy and closeness.* In: Mashek DJ, Aron AP, editors. Handbook of closeness and intimacy. Mahwah, NJ: Erlbaum; pp. 201–225.

Chapter 4

Succession Planning and Inheriting the Mantle

Introduction

With a population of more than 600 million and a nominal GDP of $2.31 trillion, ASEAN (the Association of Southeast Asian Nations), made up of Brunei Darussalam, Myanmar, Cambodia, Indonesia, Laos, Malaysia, Philippines, Singapore, Thailand and Vietnam, is fast becoming a major economic force in Asia and a driver of global growth. The economies of China and India, at the time of writing this book, are not in good shape and the GDPs are lowering for the last few years. Post Covid-19, US investors are expected to invest aggressively in this region and also many corporations from the western world may shift their manufacturing facilities here as many news items quote. The ASEAN Economic Community is also drawing plans to integrate the regional economies to make the countries more competitive with the rest of the world[1].

ASEAN member states combined with China and India could be very powerful economically. However, the challenges are large, and each of these countries has the task of building policies, infrastructure, manpower, and other resources. In such scenarios, the statistics seem to be going in favour of family businesses in Asia.

As ASEAN grows, recent research shows the region now receives more foreign direct investment (FDI) inflows than China. In 2013, Indonesia, Malaysia, the Philippines, Singapore and Thailand, known as the ASEAN-5 countries, received $128.4 billion in foreign investment, up by 7% from the previous year and topping China's FDI receipts of $117.6 billion, which declined 2.9% from 2012. Southeast Asia overtakes China in foreign direct investments.

In other words, there are great opportunities for Asian business. These opportunities are clearly an advantage to family business companies. I foresee as an author, consultant and researcher, that family business in Asia will gain the most out of this positive outlook by the investors and the FDI flow into Asia.

When we say, "Family business/firm/enterprise", what image comes to your mind? A business, that is taken care of by a father and mother or sometimes carried on over the second generation and serves a local market? The story is otherwise. The fact is that just over half of the 30 biggest firms in 27 developed countries are family-owned, according to a Forbes report (December 19, 2017)[2].

As the statistics indicate, more than 90% of business houses and small and medium sector companies are family owned business. It has been a fact that family businesses are more profit oriented than the public companies.

It is difficult to overstate the importance of the longevity and stability of Asian family businesses for the region – around 85 percent of businesses in Southeast Asia valued at $1 billion or more are founder- or family-run; in India, that figure stands at 67 percent, while in China, it is 40 percent. The 15 wealthiest families in Hong Kong control assets worth 84 percent of Hong Kong's GDP; in Malaysia, they control

76 percent, and in Singapore, just fewer than 50 percent. (Susan and Sunitha, 2017)[3].

Why Are Family Businesses Important?

Family businesses are quite different from publicly listed companies. The first distinguishing characteristic is that they are free from the pressures of shareholders, and so can genuinely think and act with longer term perspectives. One necessary driver for longer-term thinking in family business is that no generation wants to be the one that kills the business. But more than survival, family firms almost universally want to generate goodness alongside wealth. Most of them want to support and build their communities. The research supported by the United Overseas Bank (UOB) *Riding on Asia's Economic Transformation – Growth Strategies of Asian Business Families*, that balancing growth with stability is the top priority for four out of five Asian business families. The emphasis on stability stems from the desire to protect and serve family members, employees, suppliers, customers and the local community. Business owners are keenly aware that the viability of the business is closely linked to the livelihoods of many, and thus, needs to be sustainable for the benefit of all stakeholders.

I have taken a report from Europe to compare with the Asian family business scenario. The attempt is to express the importance of family business across the globe and their significant contribution to nation development in terms of GDP, employment generation and wealth creation.

The European Family Businesses forum in its research (2009)[4], into family businesses, have indicated the family business enterprises have significant benefits to the economy and to society at large:

- Most studies show that in terms of accounting performance, family businesses are more profitable over the long term.

- Family businesses are less likely to lay people off and more likely to hire.
- Family businesses are generally better for the communities in which they live; and they invest more in their communities, both for business investment and in terms of philanthropic activities.
- Family businesses generally take a long-term view and thus balance.
- Short-term rewards with long term sustainability and prosperity.
- Family businesses incur less debt and are therefore more stable.

I see certain commonalities between European and Asian family research outcomes. The family run Businesses focus in both continents are same in terms of giving importance to sustainability, interest in community development, long term vision, and also the interest in passing the business to the next generation as common.

However, family businesses also have vulnerabilities;

- Around the world, family businesses typically have successful transitions at the rate of 30% per generation which means that 30% make it in the family from first to second generation, 10% from second to third generation, 3% from third to fourth and fewer than 1% from fourth to fifth and beyond.

Research findings suggest that more than 80% of business corporations and small businesses are a family business. According to the best available research, the importance of family business has been reflected in:

- GDP - in most countries around the world they generate 60 - 90% of non-governmental GDP.
- Jobs - in most countries around the world they provide 50 – 80% of all private sector jobs.
- Start-Ups - 85% of all business start-ups are started with family money.

- Job growth - in the United States, family businesses represent more than 75% of net job growth.

One additional question which may need to be answered is: "Do they outperform non-family counterparts in business?" The answer lies in understanding the family characteristics and designing a successful sequential plan for the next generation.

Succession Planning - The Way Forward

The same as I stated in the previous paragraph, that family businesses in Asia and Europe are keen to develop a strategy for handing over to the next generation and how they can outperform nonfamily businesses. I take the concept from the book written by Grant Walsh (2011) for KPMG that captures the essence of outperforming characters of family business. He calls those characteristics as "Family Components." It would appear that the unique characteristic of family business, and the potential benefits derived from this unique characteristic, can provide a significant competitive advantage. If these family components are taken care of while designing a succession plan, then there is no chance of the plan to fail.

Grant (2011)[5] writes that professional advisers to family owned and operated businesses need to acknowledge that they are in part responsible for the dismal performance experienced by family businesses in succession. It has been found through various studies that lots of attention is given to the technical component of succession (e.g., tax minimization, estate freezes, family trusts, buy-sell agreements, wealth management, etc.) and too little attention has been given to the people, or non-technical, component (family communication, family expectations, family values, family competencies, family dynamics, etc.) in the succession planning process. We will refer to the "people" or "non-technical" component of the family business succession process as the "family component."

"While the majority of family business owners would like to see their business transferred to the next generation, it is estimated that 70% will not survive into the 2nd generation and 90% will not make it to the 3rd generation[6]."

So why are these same family businesses struggling with the transition process? Once again, the unique characteristic of family business (the family component) and the challenges it can create, if left unmanaged, are often responsible for these business failures.

Impact of the Family Component on the Business

The Three Circle Model (Taguiri and Davis, 1982)[7] outlined below is often used to illustrate the interaction/impact of the family component on the management and ownership of family businesses. The Three Circle Model is represented by the ownership circle, the management circle, and the family circle.

Three Circle Model

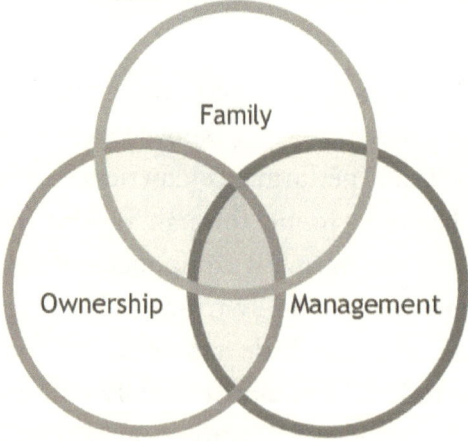

The ownership circle represents the interaction/impact that the *owners* have on the family and on the management of the business. The management circle represents the interaction/impact that *management* has on the family and on the ownership of the business. The family circle represents the interaction/impact that the *family* has on the management and ownership of the business.

The ownership circle and the management circle are common to all businesses. ***The family circle is unique to family business and is what differentiates it from its non-family business counterparts.*** In many family businesses, the family permeates the management and the ownership of the business, making it a significant, if not the major component in the overall running of the family business. It is easy to see how the interaction between these three components can create family, management, and ownership challenges, as well as provide unique opportunities.

The Three Circle Model illustrates how each of the components interacts with each other and how all three circles meet in the middle, indicating that in some respect, in the family business ownership, management, and family are mixed together.

The three-circle model by Taguiri and Davis (1982) is a powerful model to explain the influence of family on ownership and management. If we draw any circle bigger than the other two, one can explain who influences the other two. However, in family business situation the family circle is always bigger and its influence on the other two components are significant and especially when the family is multigenerational. In effect, in many family businesses, the ownership is all family and the management is all or primarily family. In these situations, learning how to effectively manage the family component is even more important.

The ability of family businesses to outperform their non-family counterparts and successfully transfer the business to the next generation is very much dependent on their ability to manage their 'family component'.

The Three Circle Model

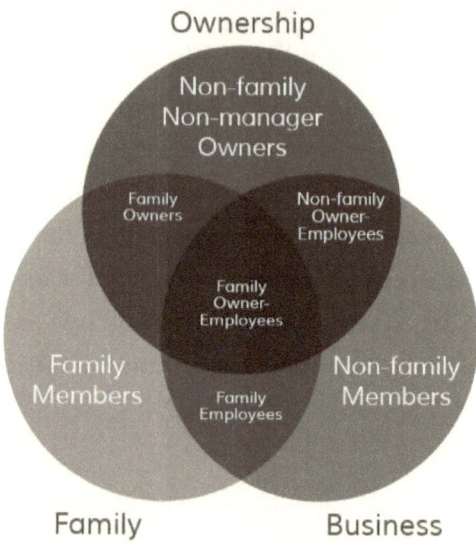

The above detailed model by Taguiri and Davis (1982)[7] became, and continues to be, the central organizing framework for understanding family business systems, used by families, consultants and academics worldwide.

This framework clarifies, in simple terms, the three interdependent and overlapping groups that comprise the family business system: family, business and ownership. As a result of this overlap, there are seven interest groups present, each with its own legitimate perspectives, goals and dynamics. The long-term success of family business systems depends on the functioning and mutual support of each of these groups.

In summary, I have identified that what makes family business different from non-family business is the 'family component'. This unique family business characteristic brings both challenges and opportunities. Family businesses need to commit to managing their family component, and the first step in doing this is being aware of, and staying in touch with, what is going on in the field of family business as well as what is going on in the family.

The family firm is a particularly prevalent form of ownership in the Asia-Pacific region, accounting for 85 percent of businesses. Some of these family firms are among the largest in the world, such as the Pacific Construction Group Company Ltd, (China) Samsung Electronics (South Korea), Reliance Industries (India) and Chow Tai Fook (Hong Kong), Bakrie & Brothers, (Indonesia), DMCI Holdings, (The Philippines), Genting Group, (Malaysia), Hero MotoCorp, (India), and Tat Hong Holdings, (Singapore), to cite only a few.

Having stated that highly successful companies in Asia that how do they have their successful existence for more than two or three generations, the obvious logical question one may ask; how did they manage the business successfully for so long? The answer lies in designing a successful Leadership and Succession Plan.

Succession Planning in Family Business

Succession planning is always a challenging, though essential, process in a family business environment, especially, when there are multiple siblings, multiple generations, and more cousins. In my personal consulting experience with a large family, two brothers and a sister are involved in the business as the second generation. The issue of conflict arose concerning the inclusion of the brother in law as a director, by the founder, as he was very fond of his daughter. (Though most commonly, daughters are not invited to be in the business in India. It's the same in many places across the world. However, in some of the subcultures in South India, daughters are given equal shares in business too). Due to this inclusion, the second generation in this company is undergoing tremendous amounts of conflict and stress.

The second example comes from the famous business conglomerate, Murugappa Group in India, which has become a role model in bringing "best practices" into family businesses. They are currently in a legal battle with the past chairman's daughter as she is demanding a board position in case, they are not bought out of their shares of the market value of the inherited shares from the father. The family says, women will not be inducted into the business (Business Today, January 18, 2020)[8]. Despite their proactive actions to manage the family business, still there is a challenge in progressing smoothly. Therefore, it is important to understand that to nurture the dream or vision of the family to run a business organization for several generations and centuries, it requires lots of attention on succession planning.

Before we jump into succession planning, there are several things one has to address seriously to bring the best possible succession plan into reality.

It is quoted in an article based on the STEP 2019 Global Family Business Survey[9], for family-owned business leaders, the good news is that their millennial children are ready to take over the family business. The not-so-good news is that over 70 per cent of family businesses do not have a formal succession plan in place. This deficiency is further complicated by the fact that the younger generation tends to want to retire earlier – often by age 50 – most current leaders plan to stay on after age 60, with some into their 70s. This trend represents a major disconnect and can create lesions between generations," says Mario Paron, Canadian managing partner, KPMG Enterprise. "It shows that important conversations about succession planning aren't happening but need to."

According to the Smith Family Business Initiative at Johnson Cornell University website report, the numbers reveal very interesting insights. Though the data are about the USA, there is still some learning for us in Asia. The data indicate;

- 32% of family businesses were apprehensive about the transfer of the business to the next generation, and 9% see the possibility of family conflict as a result (PwC Family Business Survey 2012)[10].
- The average lifespan of a family-owned business is 24 years (familybusinesscenter.com, 2010)[11]. About 40% of U.S. family-owned businesses turn into second-generation businesses,

approximately 13% are passed down successfully to a third generation, and 3% to a fourth or beyond (Businessweek.com, 2010)[11].

Learning from the above data, it is imperative to know whether the children in the family are willing to take up the role in the family company or not, as they may nurture their own dreams to do something different. Based on all the above data and information I say that, "now is the time to start a conversation on succession planning for family business"

In general, from my experience of consulting and reading, the children in the family business may be categorized into three types: Aspirants, Anchors and Explorers.

The *Aspirants* are always ambitious, and demonstrate qualities such as energy driven, committed, passionate, of high entrepreneurial spirit, want to build institutions, and set a high pace of growth, carry forward core family values, seek recognition for performance, believe that they are the best, that they are marketable, and view the family business as opportunities to charter their own courses, seek freedom to work, and resist equality within family that lacks the criterion of merit. These are the people to be observed and nurtured, as they are wealth creators for the family and the family must nurture them for leadership development and succession.

The *Anchors*, on the other hand, exhibit qualities such as being highly committed to the business and the family; viewing themselves as intrinsic parts of the family business; subscribing to core values; seeking to participate in running the business; and focusing on efficiency of operations, value status, security, and the perks/infrastructure that business provides. These qualities will help the organization and management to strengthen its systems and processes. Therefore, they must be given an appropriate position in the business to leverage their commitment and strengths, and to give management depth to the family business. They are the potential candidates for becoming a Chairman of the company to anchor the business to stabilize and grow, slowly but steadily.

The third type of children, **Explorers**, (sometimes I like to call them "Deviators") generally have their key interests outside of the business, with little or no interest or inclination towards the business; placing low value on the status, perks and infrastructure that the business provides; seeking support from the business to fund their interests; wanting to reserve the opportunity for their offspring to join the business in the future, and hence they force themselves into operations management, or may also pursue other interests in life such as photography, research, devotion to God, philanthropy, and so on.

Families or family councils must understand the above types of interests among the children first hand and decide to design the succession planning accordingly.

With the above understanding and identifying the right child for succession within the family business, then the family council may plan a succession plan.

Walsh (2011)[5], suggests a well thought out model for planning a succession and how to go about it. The model is described below:

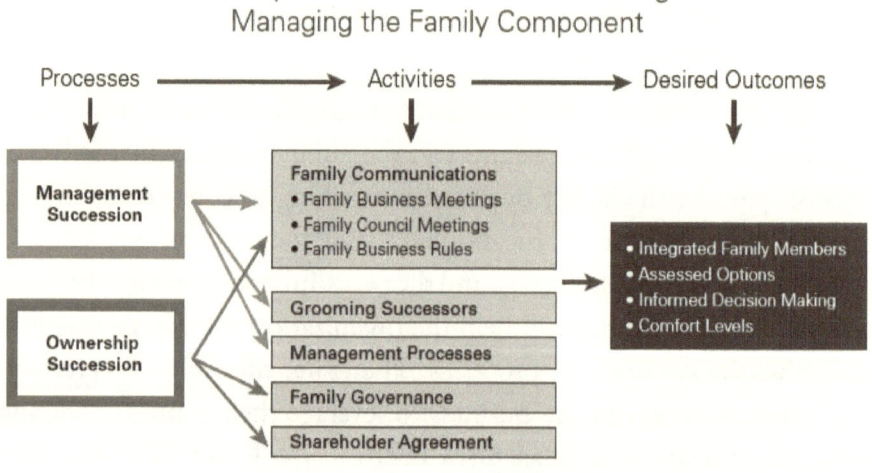

(Reproduced with permission from Grant Walsh, 2011)

Succession Processes

The family business succession plan comprises two processes, the 'management' succession process and the 'ownership' succession process. Numerous succession activities are outlined for each of the two processes to achieve the desired succession outcomes. The management and ownership succession processes can be undertaken simultaneously or one at a time. It is recommended that the management succession process be carried out first, so that the ownership succession plan reflects and supports the management succession.

There are several examples available on the management succession plans, executed first and ownership succession plan next. Many families bring the son/daughter into the payroll of the company first to begin a role at the work floor or at the lower rank. The management succession plan will be a super-fast track, where the incumbent has to learn from each step and move up in the ladder quickly to assume a top management position in a few years, generally from 3 - 5 years' time. This exercise is carried out to give a firsthand experience about the human resources, certain practices specific to the company, systems & processes involved, understanding how the structure works and also the technology aspects of business.

Succession Activities

The model shows a number of family business succession activities intended to integrate family members into the management and ownership succession processes. The activities are also anticipated to make family members feel comfortable with both the succession process and its outcomes. The ultimate goal is to allow family members to make informed decisions about their individual and collective futures in the management and ownership of the family business.

Establishing family communication activities, such as family business meetings for the active family members, family council meetings for the broader family, and family business rules, will serve to guide the overall succession process. These communication activities will pave the way for the effective management of the all-important family component. The management succession activities also include the grooming of successors and integrating the active family members into a number of key management activities.

The model also shows the ownership succession process including a list of succession activities involving family members. These activities comprise the same channels of communication as indicated in the management succession process. The ownership succession activities also include family governance and shareholder agreement issues.

The management and ownership succession activities can be carried out simultaneously. However, it is recommended that the management succession process/plan be underway or in place before undertaking the ownership succession activities. You will notice that the proposed activities to manage the family's communication (family business meetings, family council meetings, and the family rules) are the same for both the management and ownership succession processes. What will differ is the type of succession issues that are addressed at the family meetings. It is strongly recommended that regardless of which of the management or ownership succession processes are undertaken, you start with the family communication activities.

Desired Outcomes

The succession activities outlined in the above model are intended to achieve the desired succession outcomes. By integrating family members into the process and by providing sufficient comfort to the current and future owners of the family business, informed decisions can be made. It is these informed decisions that will ensure a smooth and effective family business transition.

If the current owners are not sufficiently comfortable with the proposed financial arrangements, the management succession plan, or the ownership succession plan, they will most likely not let go. The owners have invested far too much in the family business to pass it on without the necessary assurances that it will continue to prosper. Furthermore, the owners want to be assured that the family and key employees, often referred to as the extended family, are also taken care of. The same can be said for the next generation. If the next generation is not sufficiently comfortable with the proposed roles and responsibilities of the management succession team, the compensation philosophy, the distribution of wealth, and the funding of the ownership transition, they will most likely delay or defer their willingness to implement a succession plan. Therefore, the sooner the succession activities get underway, the more opportunity there is for each party to build their comfort zones.

The higher the comfort levels of those involved, the easier it is for them to make decisions. The speed at which the succession process unfolds will be in large part based on the owner's knowledge of their options and their level of comfort, both of which will lead to informed decisions. Therefore, developing the succession process with activities that will provide options, assess comfort, and allow for informed decision making by family members is essential for success.

For the Successors - Inheriting the Mantle

Inheriting the mantle is a biblical reference stated in the book of Kings in the Bible[12]. It is about a prophet and his disciple. The prophet Elijah comes to know that it was time for him to go (leave the earth) so he informs his disciple, Elisha. The Prophet had a lot of powers. The disciple asks for a double portion of his blessing. So, when the prophet was taken to heaven his shawl (referred as mantle) fell on the disciple Elisha and he used it as a sign and performed greater miracles than this master. It is in the Book of Kings in the Bible. As the reference goes, it is also important for the successors to inherit the wealth and business from the parents, also along with the values and cultures which they have built the business over the years. Like Elisha the Prophet, the inheritor also must be able to perform better, showing brilliant competencies than the parents in business. Therefore, the next generations need to focus on learning, developing necessary skills and acquiring the business acumen from the family to do a lot superior. What are the ways to make the next generation ready to inherit?

Let me share my current experience of working with the family business client. The client is having a business in Polymer packaging solutions company and has a manufacturing facility and has ambitions to grow to 100 million over next 8 years in other sectors such as agriculture and automobiles or manufacturing. The business is being managed by two brothers and they have two children each. The elder brother has a daughter and son and the younger one has two sons. The two sons of the brothers or the cousins of the same age are studying graduate engineering. The family council has decided to bring them to the business in the next 8 years' time. We have already drawn the road map on how to get them into the business and hand over the company to them. Before we designed the road map this aspect also is addressed in the family constitution that they have to earn this position by merit and not by legal status.

The Road Map

1. Both the sons were given an orientation on the family constitution and we gave them awareness to qualify to take over the business.
2. Both of them must have a master's degree, preferably from a foreign university in a relevant field.
3. Must have a minimum of three years working experience in other companies, or a three year on the job training program is designed with the fast track succession planning within the family business.
4. They will be under a performance monitoring program during this period.

5. Once they complete the process, they will be assessed through business plans, vision building and managerial ability to strengthen the existing systems or will be funded for a new project which they propose.

The above is a tentative schedule and time frame but it's dynamic. I work with both the sons and coach them to get ready to inherit the mantle. It's a long-drawn process and the family is willing to invest time and money on this as they firmly believe that this exercise is important.

In Picture : Padma Vibushan Shri. Ramesh Mashelkar, Myself and Dr BorizCizelj, The Chairman of (KEN), at the podium

The above picture was taken when I was invited and delivered a lecture in Family Business Network, in New Delhi, promoted by the Confederation of Indian Industry (CII) sponsored by Knowledge Economy Network (KEN) from Belgium. The interesting part of the presentation was, when I started speaking on succession planning, the audience, most of them were next generation entrepreneurs, not showed any interest in the presentation. Noticing this indifference after a few minutes I asked them, 'why they were not interested"? They expressed very interesting issues which they face with the elders in the family.

They said they have learnt enough about succession planning and the elder generation or the fathers are not willing to allow them to function completely. So, they brought out a view that the fathers are the ones that need this training and not them. Then I changed the course of the topic on the "Inheriting the mantle". I was astonished to find that the hall was getting full and they became keen listeners. Because I presented such content how they can get ready on their own to inherit the business.

Summary

I want to conclude this chapter with an understanding that the succession planning is not a one-way process and it is a two-way process. Handing over the business and taking over must happen smoothly. The elderly generation needs to prepare to induct the next generation and train them until they are ready and move gracefully over the years. Ideally, they should retire from the business in about 8 years from the next generation is ready to step in. They may continue as advisors or mentors to them to give guidance for some time, but they should be prepared to hand over the authority to the next generation within this time period. Otherwise, the younger generation would feel that they are taken into mistrust and will lose confidence to take the business forward. They may lose motivation over a period of time. That would be a potential loss to the family.

Reference

1. http://www.channelnewsasia.com/news/business/international/southeast-asia-overtakes/1021378.html)

2. Forbes Report (2017) https://www.forbes.com/sites/nusbusinessschool/2017/12/19/3-myths-about-family-businesses-and-their-role-in-asias-economies/#59a654d51b8a

3. Susan ho and Sunitha chalam (2017) *A New Wave*, Brunswick review · issue 11

4. Final Report of the Expert Group, *'Overview of Family-Business-Relevant-Issues: Research, Networks, Policy Measures and Existing Studies'* (November 2009), http://www.europeanfamilybusinesses.eu/uploads/Modules/Publications/family-business-statistics.pdf

5. Grant Walsh (2011) *Family Business Succession, Managing the All-Important Family Component*, KPMG

6. www.isb.edu

7. https://johndavis.com/family-resilience-in-the-time- of corona/?utm_source=rss&utm_medium=rss&utm_campaign=family-resilience-in-the-time-of-corona

8. *Murugappa group family feud: It's time for more women to join family businesses*, Business Today, January 18, 2020.

9. Calabrò, Andrea & Valentino, Alfredo (2019), *STEP2019 Global Family Business Survey - REPORT The impact of changing demographics on family business succession planning and governance.*

10. *PwC Family Business Survey (2012), Family firm The India perspective*, https://www.pwc.in/assets/pdfs/family-business-survey/family-business-survey-2013.pdf

11. Family Business Facts, https://www.johnson.cornell.edu/smith-family-business-initiative-at-cornell/resources/family-business facts/#:~:text=Business%20Survey%202012).-,The%20average%20life%20span%20of%20a%20family%2Downed%20business%20is,Businessweek.com%2C%202010).

12. https://biblehub.com/context/2_kings/2-7.htm

13. *Southeast Asia overtakes China in foreign direct investments;* http://www.channelnewsasia.com/news/business/international/southeast-asia-overtakes/1021378.html

Chapter 5

Family Constitution and Building Institutions

Introduction

In my two decades of consulting experience, I have apprised, suggested enough measures to improvise all companies that range from startups to large well-established ones, both in India and in a few other countries. I identified a pattern that is common among these companies about how they grow from a startup or an entrepreneurial venture into a large business house. Also, I learned how some companies have remained undersized for the last two decades without growth. Some of the companies have grown and transformed successfully from ownership driven to professionally driven companies through the leadership and decision-making process by the founders.

I was invited to consult to one of the well-established construction companies in 2005 in a town called Erode, in Tamil Nadu in India. When I was invited by the then Director and current Joint Chairman, Mr. Devarajan, the company was doing a business worth approximately USD8 million at the then existed rate of international exchange. Devarajan, as a second-generation entrepreneur, following the footsteps of his father in the family business, entered the business with a vision of making the company into an USD100 million enterprise. Though everything was set for his entry and performance, the challenges came from different corners, including the family, as the founder always wanted his sons to be living better and to find a stress-free life. He used to advise them that he has made enough wealth to live peacefully and harmoniously with the family and society, and therefore, he was not for scaling up the business. However, Devarajan, as a self-driven man, decided to build the business, beyond what his father had created – to create more; and that could turn out to be the right tribute to reward his father. He convinced his father and started taking steps towards growth of the business. I was invited by him as a consultant and we started working on the organization structure, writing and laying down the HR policies for compensation and other benefits, career and succession planning and more. We also identified the right person for the right job within the organization to start with and later started recruiting laterally. I designed an intervention manual for vision building, leadership, motivation and implementing systems & processes. We named it as *"Vision – 250"*, the expression simply made for achieving Rs.250 crores of business in 3 years (i.e., close to USD30 Million). I realized during this consulting process if the company is to transform, the leader must also transform and be willing to go through the processes of change of both self and organization. I call this a crucible experience. Mr. Devarajan, having decided to scale up his business took on all challenges and sailed successfully to achieve Rs.250 crores business in 4 years (in 2009). I portray this experience to emphasize the point that leadership matters for business and organization growth. As a second-generation entrepreneur he is able to scale and sustain the business growth. In the process, the organization size and number of employees also have grown up. Currently the URC Construction Group is performing as a USD 130 Million company with 1400 staff and 7000 contract employees, with its presence in ''11 states" in India. The group is not only grown up with the business turn over, but it is standing tall with brand name, and as an established institution. It is now being managed by the third generation at the forefront and Mr. Devarajan and other Directors are driving the business from the board.

Now Mr. Devarajan desires to make the company as a multigenerational one and wanted to build it from the organization to an institution, 'so that the company can live longer for centuries and upcoming generations will run the business 'he reveals. Not all organizations are able to meet all the challenges in the business environment; more so, do they have the leadership necessary to drive growth successfully? Family business in general, I understand, when I talk to the owners, I see the interest in them to build business organizations or institutions to several generations and centuries. In simple terms of understanding, the family business owners want to build "Long Living Companies."

What made them different from other companies in the region? They had foresight on business opportunities, desire to grow, leadership and managerial competencies and good management of the family and business.

The list of long living companies in the world includes about 3000 companies. Many of these are located in Japan, Germany and in the US[1].

Also, among the top 750 family companies across the world, the survey reported by Family Capital prepared by David Bain (2019)[1], is clearly noting the Asian dominance of family businesses on the list. In the report it is mentioned, as quoted by Peter Englisch, a global family business leader for Price Waterhouse Coopers (PwC),

"The global shift of power is now also reflected in the ranking of the world's leading family businesses," he says. "America is still going to dominate the index, but the rise of the Asian family businesses put

European leaders under pressure to maintain a leading position in the future."

Out of the 750 companies, 57 were from China (16 based in Hong Kong and 41 from mainland China). This number compares well with Germany, perhaps the country with the most advanced family enterprise culture, with 119 companies on the list.

The data clearly establishes the power of Asian businesses in the region, which generates annual revenues of more than USD 9 trillion. These companies employ nearly 30 million people.

There is one more set of data about the longevity of the multinational organizations. The multinational business conglomerates average life expectancy (Fortune 500 or its equivalent) is between 40 and 50 years. This figure is based on most surveys of corporate births and deaths. A full one-third of the companies listed in the 1970 Fortune 500, for instance, had vanished by 1983—acquired, merged, or broken to pieces. The average human life span has increased to 75 years while there are few companies that are that old and flourishing.

When I started writing this chapter on building institutions, I was looking for some data to justify my idea about why some companies progress and live longer and others don't. I came across an interesting book called the Living Company - Growth, Learning and Longevity in Business, written by Arie de Geus (1997). He published this book after carrying out research for the company he worked for, The Shell Group. The research was to identify the long living companies and the reasons for their long-term success. He and his fellow researchers ended up with a few components that made these companies live longer is:

- *Sensitivity to the environment* represents a company's ability to learn and adapt.
- *Cohesion and identity are* aspects of a company's innate ability to build a community and a persona for itself.

- *Tolerance, and its corollary, decentralization*, is both symptoms of a company's awareness of ecology: its ability to build constructive relationships with other entities, within and outside itself.
- *Conservative financing* as one element in a very critical corporate attribute: the ability to govern its own growth and evolution effectively.

The above four components represent a kind of a guideline (though I am not presenting it as a panacea for longevity of organizations) for other companies to follow.

In present-day Europe, a sizable number of firms are 200 or more years old. In fact, there were so many such firms in the United Kingdom that they had their own trade association, the Tercentenaries' Club, which only accepts member companies, over 300 years old. It is understood that many of them are still under the control of the founding family dynasty. That means the families are able to transfer the business, organization and wealth to the next generations successfully for a long period and across multiple generations.

When the desire of Devarajan to build an organization worth USD 100 million (currently more than that) was achieved, what must be his next goal? I asked him what his next goal is and his answer is instructive and interesting.

"How does one hand over the family business to the next generation and also prepare them to be successful and eventually hand over to their children, so that the organization becomes a "living company"?

These kinds of conversations make me feel confident about my hypothesis that each founder wanted the business to grow and live for multiple generations.

I have another client who comes from the same town that I have been helping in their Family Business Management for the last four years, called CD Group. The founder started an edible oil business in the 1970s and became a well-known oil producer and supplier across the South and West Indian region. Massive business and wealth were built over three decades. His brother also was taking care of some responsibilities and played a critical role in managing the business. However, the sudden demise of the founder, at an early age, created lots of conflict in terms of succession within the family. After some time, the family split apart, and the oil business was closed. Currently the cousins have divided the businesses and manage it separately.

With this background and experience, the founder's first son Mr. Kumar, educated in the US, is eager to proactively take steps to avoid any future conflicts and wanted to carry on the business with the younger brother as a family business. He invited me to write a family constitution, family governance, create a family council and want to practice the best family business practices. In the diagnosis process, we clearly understood that writing the *Family Constitution* is the best way to avoid many future conflicts. We have completed this constitution document, capturing almost all areas from building family vision, values of the founder and family, employee management practices, family role in business, and the extent of acceptable and unacceptable behaviors of family members. Though the family constitution document is not legally binding, it still serves as a guiding document to prepare the next generation. Many of my clients, and also members of my professional circle, share the same opinion that are in an order for families to go a long way and build a living company, they need to have a clear and agreed upon family constitution that sets forth relevant rules and family business policies.

Swati Sharma (2019)[3], in her article for Asian Age magazine, wrote:

"Disagreements, if not managed well and in a timely fashion, are sure to lead to conflict. And, any conflict within the family impacts the business negatively".

"You can't say conflicts are more or less in a family or non-family business. It all depends on what you call a conflict. In a non-family context, employees have a clear exit route which is not the case with a family business. Families have to discuss and develop policies for various issues covering ownership, rewards, retirement, rights, duties and responsibilities, all of which lead to the creation of a family constitution. They should start the exercise as early as possible," explains Kavil Ramachandran, Professor at Indian Business School[3].

He further quotes that "No wonder then Indian business families are now scripting family constitutions to avoid drama later on. Apollo Hospitals, the GMR group, Burmans and Emami are just some of the family businesses that have put constitutions in place".

The family constitution of the Apollo Hospitals Group was drafted after several discussions and signed by all the family members and the Chairman. "At Apollo, the family constitution has been signed by all three generations with succession planning and clarity of roles as well. The crux of making this successful transition understands that businesses exist for the customers, that our employees depend on the company's success for their livelihood and that a corporate legacy must be protected".

The company's interests must be placed ahead of the family member's interests every time. It is not easy to do, if the spirit is imbibed into the family from the very beginning, as has been done in ours, then good corporate governance comes naturally," adds Sangita[3].

The GMR group also took all the family members on a retreat to understand each one's relationships within the group. They laid out a code of conduct and rules for every family member's entry into the business.

In Malaysia the family business practices are also well captured in the literature, mostly by the consulting company publications. A PWC report (family business survey 2018)[4] shared some very interesting information: 58% of family businesses are prepared to discuss family conflicts. However, the family council and constitution still rank below the global standards and only 13% family businesses have the constitution or protocol in Malaysia; 68% of them with no next generation notion in their business plan to pass on management and/or ownership to the next generation.

Mostly 75% of those already have next generation family members working in the business, and there are plans in place to pass on management and or ownership to the next generation. These families, when they pass the management or ownership to the next generation, it will greatly help if these families proactively create family constitution documentation and other policies in writing. That shows there is a huge potential for the family businesses in Malaysia to consider developing the family constitution or protocol for family members.

The family constitution defines the "rules of the road" for the family with respect to its relationship to the business. In simple terms, a family constitution can be thought of as a collection of key family policies. It would also reflect the vision, mission and values of the family and important principles for working together for the business.

It could also include a description of the composition and role of the family council, and how the family council makes decisions and resolves conflicts. It could include a description of the other governance structures that go to make up the family business (or the wider family enterprise if you make reference to the family foundation and the family office, for example). There is no fixed definition and there is no one way to do it. Here are some more descriptions of what a family constitution is by experts:

"A Family Constitution is a formal document developed collaboratively by family members to encapsulate the values, beliefs and objectives of the family, as a family, with specific reference to the family's relationship and dealing with its family business." Ivan Lansberg (1999)[5]

"A Family Constitution is "… a legal or quasi legal, guide for family behaviour, decision-making, and setting up the succession from one generation to another. Beginning with the mission statement, the constitution then extends the mission into practical actions. It sets up a framework and a forum for a group of equals to deliberate issues, create policies and Procedures, clearly define family member's rights and obligations, and make decisions about the important issues they share." Dennis T. Jaffe, (2014)[6].

Having given a long background for the importance of having a family constitution, now it is time to learn how the policies are being developed for family businesses. In fact, I propose that along with Arie de Geus (1997)[2] findings of four components of living companies, I propose the fifth component that is family constitution.

Writing Family Constitution

After discussing the fundamentals of family constitution drafting and writing it requires care. Recalling my conversation with Mr. Kumar of CD group, which I referred earlier paragraph, in our first meeting, we call it as "First Contact" and subsequently "Chemistry Meeting" (Davis and Dyer, 2003)[7], and he mentioned the following.

"We have had a great business but failed to have methods of working on the conflicts among the family members, when my father was alive. Because everything was going well once he was alive, and everyone followed his instructions and direction. But his sudden demise brought different dynamics and now we are keen to have the best practices to run the family and business without conflicts. We needed policies to guide our family members and the business and that would bring the role of boundaries clearly".

He was looking for solutions proactively for the future problems and after four years our client- consultant relationship is still moving strong with an establishment of family constitution, business policies and many more interventions designed for the organizational growth.

It is important that the leader of the family realizes the need for writing the constitution and convince other siblings and family members to have a constitution.

Like Kumar, I wish all other family businesses to have vision and foresight to put things in place before any crisis hits. The best way for family businesses to avoid problems is to create family business policies.

Policies must bring clarity among the family members on their relationship at business and decision-making processes.

We need to keep it in mind that if you compare a family business constitution writing of two families it won't be similar. Because it all depends on the family size, generations in the family and business, values and culture, vision and mission of the business, charity attitude, wealth etc.

Therefore, the first step is to invite all eligible adult members of the family for a huddle, preferably an offsite meeting, facilitated by an outside consultant.

Based on several case studies of Indian businesses, particularly because I have only Indian clients, I like to generate a few questions as a first step to ask in the family gathering/meeting. Those are:

- When is the next generation step into the business?
- What merits or qualifications they should possess?
- What kind of challenges is expected in the future in terms of succession planning, dividend pay-outs, and role allocations in the business?
- Can anyone borrow money or take a loan from the business?
- When will I earn a board position?
- What will I do if I have a question that may cause a potential conflict in the family?
- What would be the role of my wife in the business?
- I am the eldest of the family; therefore will I become a chairman of the group automatically?
- How is the compensation defined for the family member who is taking care of the business?
- How to recruit a relative in the business organization? What are the criteria?
- Can I take a sabbatical from business to upgrade my skills in business or pursue my other interests for a while?

We need to generate as many as such questions in the meeting and each one may contribute by thinking from all angles of the potential family issues. Once these questions are listed, then one by one each of the questions need to be addressed and possible focus pointers to be developed for family constitution.

This exercise helps the family members mentally be prepared for the future challenges and think from the perspectives of solutions than problem solving.

Once these questions are jointly addressed and debated among the family members, then the next process would be to start drafting the policies based on the topics/areas. According to Aronoff et al., (2011)[8] the following must be kept in mind. They advise start with easier policies;

Easier	Harder	Hardest
Employment (when not facing anytime soon)	Compensation	Governance (Family Council and board directors)
Code of Conduct	Publicity	Shareholder agreements
Philanthropy	Dividends	Conflicts of interests

Policies in general, in our understanding, give direction to make decisions. It also helps the decision maker to use the policies as a ready reckoned table for self-consultation. Therefore, the constitution or business policies cannot be kept just as a rule book. It should carry the values and culture practiced by the founder of the first family of the business.

In the CD Group case, we have decided that the family constitution is the best way to direct the family members and business. In order to bring out the essence of the founder's value, we began our work in doing a content analysis of the founders' work, his values through evidence which is a collection from the family members, friends, relatives, and long-term employees. It is very interesting to find his business acumen, competence on prediction of business opportunities (especially in the edible oil industry, today we call this as business analytics using millions of data, whereas he will make decisions based on few calls in the morning to determine the daily prices of oil), networking ability (he made friends across south and west, part of the nation and still the family maintains an excellent relationship as families) and the helping attitude, say charity mindset.

When we analyzed all the data collected the following values system very clearly emerged;

- Love for the family, relatives and community,
- Simple living and conserving,
- Business was of prime importance,
- Mutual respect to everyone,
- Learning,

- Helping (innumerable number of people was supported financially),
- Respecting the channel of business that is the supply chain,
- Respect and care for the whole supply chain (not squeezing the entire profit only by him),
- Philanthropy (established an educational institution where currently 15000 students study).

We took care of all, including all those values while drafting the family constitution. At the end, the document became an instrument which expressed almost all values practiced by the family. Now we are in the process of educating the third generation, though they have another 8 years to come to the business as they are still in graduation. The family constitution clearly quotes that they need to earn the position in the business by certain qualifications and outside working experience. They are being prepared.

What are the Policies Needed?

I worked at managerial capacity in corporate and drafted policies for HR management. My usual way of opening to write a policy manual is to begin with the Vision, Mission and Values statement for the company. I move to other important areas later. I like to advice in the same way for family constitutions as well. Bring the family together and facilitate a workshop on what they want to do and where they want to go from the current position. Capture the essence of the vision and develop a vision for the family. Once this is done, then ask an important question on how they want to achieve this vision? This question helps define the mission statement. In the same way, do the analysis based on the data and facilitates a question on values of the family? In essence, I am proposing a good family constitution manual, which must have the family's vision, mission and values. The manual probably has the following index ideally, but depends on the importance and easiness in developing that the order may change family to family:

1. Vision, Mission and Values Statement,
2. Code of Conduct for the family members,
3. Conflict of interests and expressions,
4. Employment Policies,
5. Compensation, Dividends, and Shareholding patterns,
6. Performance Evaluation,
7. Decision Making processes,
8. Family and Business Governance Policies,
9. Learning and up gradation skills of the family members and competence building,
10. Consequences of non-adherence of policies.

There are more to add to the list. However, the above are just the indicative areas for developing the constitution. There are other important areas such as shareholder agreements, Philanthropy, retirement age and processes, exit out of the family business, distribution of profit, use of family name, use of available finances (capital), family offices, family business relations and family meetings.

Summary

This chapter is written with a purpose of giving the importance of writing a family constitution (oftentimes the words constitution and policies are used interchangeably), to bring clarity among the family members on several areas such as decision-making process, leadership and succession planning. However, merely writing and keeping the constitution does not solve problems or prevent families from getting into troubles. The success of writing the constitution depends on how much each family member contributes to develop these policies, willing to accept the written procedures and practice, and understand the consequences of non-adherence. Family businesses, by adopting family constitutions also should agree that they are involved in building an institution that will thrive for a longer duration for many generations and be value based organizations for employees and society at large.

References

1. David bain, (2020) https://www.famcap.com/the-worlds-top-750-family-businesses-ranking/

2. Arie de Geus (1997), *The Living Company,* Nicholas Brealey Publishing, London

3. Swati Sharma (2019), *Constitutional family ties,* https://www.asianage.com/life/more-features/150319/constitutional-family-ties.html

4. A PWC report, family business survey (2018) (https://www.pwc.com/gx/en/services/family-business/family-business-survey-2018.html)

5. Ivan Lansberg (1999),*Succeeding Generations: Realizing the Dream of Families in Business,* Harvard Business Review Press; First Edition

6. Dennis T. Jaffe (2014): *Developing Responsible Family Leadership Across Generations*, Stewardship in Your Family Enterprise, First Edition"

7. Davis J H and Dyer W G (2003), *"Consulting to Family Businesses"* Jossey Bass/Pfeiffer, San Francisco

8. Craig E Aronoff, Joseph H Astrachan, and John L Ward, (2011) *"Developing Family Business Policies – Your Guide to the Future",* A Family Business Publication, Palgrave Macmillan NY

Chapter 6

Family Governance

Introduction

Family governance is defined as the methods, structures, processes and communication which families bring into play amongst them to manage their family business and guide their relationship with their business. A well-designed and properly implemented, family governance system can help set boundaries among the ownership; management and family as well create clarity. It also brings a greater harmony between family members, a more focused business, and easier transitions between generations. In order to bring in the family governance system, it has to be customized to each family's requirements based on the culture, values and particular family needs.

The Three Circle Model and Governance

The Three-Circle Model of the Family Business System, which I described in the first chapter, has relevance in this chapter to understand how each of the systems (family, business and ownership) works together and support. In addition, people within each system should appreciate which decisions are theirs to make and work within their boundaries. The interaction among three components of the family business system, support and the process of decision making is governance. The governance process provides direction and guidance in any situation, on the process of making decisions and it is ideally conflict and tension free. The governance system provides a forum for constructive discussion, problem solving and decisions about and to the family as it is related to the business, as well as, how the business is related to the family. In other ways, understanding family governance in a larger perspective is how it can help in many functions of the family and business.

It is well understood that the challenge to the sustainability of a family business is resolving conflicts among family members. Such conflicts may arise from decisions made by the heirs, competition among family members, or disputes over policies regarding succession, role allocation, compensation and dividends. These conflicts may impact the business decisions, subsequently lead to power struggle among family members and even ruin the business. In order to solve this problem, the concept of "family governance" arises. This concept comes to separate "family" and "business" from management; thereby the three components of family business do not come into conflicting zones. Business development, strategy, and growth plans are implemented through corporate governance structure. The family is being managed through family governance for intergenerational succession and growth.

Usually, in the first generation an established business will have the overlap of management, ownership and family. The family business gets more complicated, when the other younger generations come into the business. When the numbers increase in family members and the difference in individual capability, it is worth asking a question whether the overlap would still do well for the family. The answer is: The family governance becomes crucial, when the number of family members increases especially; the business is handed over to the third generation. On the other hand, when the business is passed down from the first generation to the second generation, or the number of potential successors is few, the selection and training of successors are more urgent than family governance.

In order to successfully govern a family business, the family needs to establish a family governance document that provides a note with clarity, unique in content, giving clear vision for the family. This document should expressly designate the family members who participate in the management of the business, the arrangement of intergenerational succession, the handling of expectations of all family members, whether they are in the management of the family business or not, and how the family will interact with the family business and the management of the family business. This process of developing and having a family governance document helps the family to resolve conflict and establish family cohesion and communication.

The Role of Family Governance

The family governance structure must help building a strong family and as well providing a platform to share, articulate and sort out the issues as and when it arises. I propose a six steps strategy for identifying, understanding and implementing a quality governance model or to write a document.

The First Step – Vision of the Company

The first step in this direction is, the family governance structure begins with setting the **vision** for the family and defines its **philosophy** towards the family's relationship with the business and the businesses' support of the family.

The CD group, which I have earlier quoted as an example, begins with developing of a vision as follows;

Vision

We, as a group are involved in businesses to build the most valuable Organizations for the benefit of all stakeholders in society including the employees, thereby becoming the most sought after group in the region.

We work towards ensuring better Education, Health, Bettering the Environment and Creating Wealth for the stakeholders with highest standards and ethical practices. We also ensure that we lead by example.

(Reproduced with the permission from the CD family, 2020).

When we captured the above vision after several rounds with the brothers Kumar and Shanmugasundaram (Shan as I call him) we drafted, debated and confronted several questions of possibilities and values and finally arrived at the above vision statement. It is the most valuable statement and sincerely being communicated to all stakeholders including family members and the employees. It is displayed in appropriate places in the organization. The vision statement unites each one in all three circles and becomes a guiding force.

The Second Step – Inculcating Values

The second step is the most important process in governance, which is to understand the **values** of the founder and the family members. It is a deep drive to know to uncover and the values by which the family and related enterprises will operate.

Identifying value is a subterranean work. It requires a lot of labor and data. Several experts suggest several ways to identify the values. One can take an online assessment, ask your close friends and relatives for the values you are known for and validate, focusing on deep emotional experiences to know which value system operates in you strongly and self-observation; sometimes it may be more. In the CD Group case, we have identified the values of the founder by analyzing the videos, where his close friends and beneficiaries talk about his qualities. Through this process we have identified the following value systems of him:

Peace Loving, Education, Health, Social Good (Philanthropy), and Wealth sharing and wealth creation for others, Hard Work, Honesty and Mutual Respect. Having identified those values, as a next step we had a series of workshops and presentations with the family members to implement the values, which are important for the family and business. In this direction to cater to the values of philanthropy, a charity foundation in the name of the founder is started, called CD Foundation.

The Third Step – Giving Education

Educating the family is the third step and the key material on the importance of having a governance document and practice as it is written about their rights and responsibilities of ownership, family history, and values. As an Organizational Development Practitioner, I facilitate several workshops for the family members in order to sensitize them on the important points of governance. A detailed study of the founder's life and important incidences at various stages are captured and written in the form of stories to inspire them. The CD family had interviewed several of the other family members, friends and relatives, sharing their experiences with the founder, which is made as a video. The video is kept as archives for the next generation education.

The Fourth Step – Succession Planning

We have discussed this in detail about the succession planning in the 4th chapter. In family governance, documents succession planning is always an important topic as this would be a conflict point among the cousins as everyone aspires and aims for the top position in the organization. In order to build a business organization for longer generations and living company, who leads the company really matters. The governance must guide the succession planning on a merit than the legal heir policy or as a culture that the eldest son gets the top post.

The Fifth Step – Defining a Decision-Making Process

A simple majority is usually required for a decision on most board matters, but good family business boards utilize a consensus style, seldom calling for a vote. This requires grooming and a well-defined induction process of the family members into the family council. Consensus is a nice word to hear but hard to practice. It is a culture within the family to be evolved and at the same time having a room for expressing a dissent or concerns, later involved in huddling for better decisions. In the whole process, the business becomes first without affecting the family harmony. The decision-making process in a family business is a separate topic and it may require another chapter on it. I try to just point to the concerned areas for making better informed decisions.

The Sixth Step – Communication

The sixth step I would suggest is **communication**. The family board, council or family meetings, every such occasion of meetings are to be conducted extremely in pleasant ambience and harmonious ways. How the agenda and questions are designed for discussion and prioritizing the topics for discussion is more important. I used to guide families when they gather, each cousins present something they are passionate about and its update, what was exciting about in last three or six months-time for them (one of the families started looking for a cousin's session of wildlife photography as he is an expert wildlife photographer and a forest wanderer) or any other likely achievements in the last few months. Later we enter the topics of easy to difficult items and have a pre note for each topic to be discussed. Communication is an art, especially with family members.

The Stages of Family Governance

Families which make decisions together are directly related to the size and configuration of the family. Before much research and guidance in family business, the families were more casual in communication and decision-making, and mostly decisions are made in an informal manner. Or the founder or the eldest in the family makes decisions and communicate to the next generations. As the family and the business grow, the need for more formal governance also evolves[1].

However, whatever the size family may be, it is better to have family governance in place much before any conflict arises. The second generation may be few, but sooner the third generation will occupy the roles in the business, where the second generation should have experience and be able to guide them. Last few decades healthcare development has increased the lifespan of human beings to an extent as the average life span is 74. On the other side, children's early marriages might shrink the generation gap. Therefore, it is very important that family businesses prepare themselves well in advance for any eventualities. For many, family governance starts with well-planned family meetings and communication among the family members. The meetings among the family members range from coffee tables to deep exploration of serious questions within the family, during a planned retreat.

I explain the various stages of family governance through a continuum ranging from simple to complex levels. It all depends on the size of the family. We say, "Two is a team and three is a crowd", in management. When the family transcends from first generation family to multiple generation governance, it heads towards into more complexity. The continuum figure below outlines different family governance stages and suitable methods, based on the increase in complexity and interaction of the family and the business. The intensity of meetings again depends on the size of the family from fewer members and fewer generations to more owners and multiple generations.

Figure: Continuum of Family Governance Stages

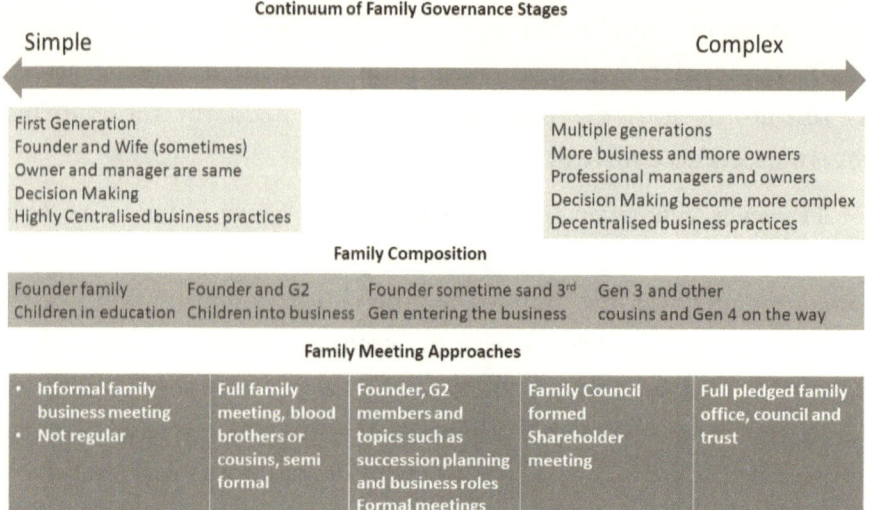

The above figure illustrates the size of the family, process of decision making, family composition and methods of meetings from simple to complex situations.

The family constitution which we have learned from the previous chapter is a document for defining and managing the family members' role, process of making decisions and various aspects of business management, whereas family governance is a process of making that constitution work. Therefore, in the family governance process it is important to have the stakeholders agreeing for the policies and guidelines and also sign it off.

Three Important Components to Family Governance

Harvard Business School (HBS) working knowledge[2] website enumerates on the important three components. However, in my experience I would add another one from my experience as many families face a situation, where the second generation doesn't even show interest to come to the father's business, due to the size of the business or by the enormous interests the second generation develops on science and technology and possibility of developing products as a business. Therefore, it is important to have a fourth component in the family governance that is, the family must have informal meetings in all possible occasions. Dyer (2019)[3] says that we are losing family capital by many factors such as marriage rates, fertility rates, divorce rates, cohabitation rates, and out of wedlock births. The first point I am making out of my experience and other three points are quotes from the work knowledge website of HBS.

1. Meet the next generation members over dining, pleasure trips and share the vision of the father (founder), stories, struggles, excitements and more. Develop and gain the interest of the next generation for preparation.

2. Periodic (typically annual) assemblies of the family to meet mostly recommended for a retreat; all family members must participate and benefit from this activity and understand the business happenings.

3. Family council meetings are an important process of family governance for the families that benefit from a representative group of their members doing planning, creating policies, and strengthening business-family communication and bondage.

4. A family constitution—is the family's policies and guiding vision and values that regulate members' relationship with the business. This written document can be short or long, detailed or simple, but every family in business benefits from this kind of document.

The family in business may have a more elaborate family governance structure, with a separate meeting for family-owner-managers or a separate council for family shareholders or periodic meetings between shareholders, the board, and management. It is preferable to have the simplest structure that does the job and the four components above are almost all most families in business need.

Properly composed and managed, a family assembly and family council help:

- Develop clarity on roles, rights, and responsibilities for family members,
- Encourage family members, family employees, and family owners to act responsibly towards the business and the family,
- Regulate appropriate family and owner inclusion in business discussions.

The family assembly typically meets annually, lasts one to two days, and includes all adult family members (yes, including in-laws, this depends on the cultures and family comforts and constitution). Family constitutions may have a clause that would provide clarity on what age children are permitted to sit in the meetings. In my experience, I find families say that they start bringing the younger generation into meetings at around the legal adult age of 18 in India.

Structures of the Family Business System

Family assembly activities include learning about the business through presentations by family and non-family managers, discussing (not deciding) the direction of the company, being educated about what the company does or about important skills like reading financial statements. It is also a good forum to get updated on changes in the family such as important events and accomplishments and also about the new tax laws shareholders need to be aware of at the business front.

If your family has fifteen or fewer adults, you may be able to have in-depth discussions and create plans and policies in the family assembly meeting. When the family grows beyond this size certainly, families generally benefit from having a family council. The family council can perform all of the following duties:

- Plan family assembly meetings.
- Discusses current business, ownership, and family issues and direction and keep the family informed about these.
- Help the family reach decisions and speak with one voice about its goals.
- Keep the board of directors informed about family views about the company and maintain a dialogue with the board about key business policies and plans.
- Develop plans and policies, in conjunction with the board, that regulate family activity with the business.
- Guard against family interference with the business while seeing that the family's key goals are satisfied.
- Develop loyal, informed, contributing family shareholders.
- Scout the family for business talent.
- Create educational events or otherwise encourage the education of family members about the business.
- Plan family social gatherings and rituals and help to create healthy, harmonious family relationships.

Any family council that accomplishes these tasks strengthens a family's relationship with its business and its discipline and is a valuable resource for management and the board.

The family council can be composed in several ways, the typical way being one member elected per family branch. One should try to compose the family council so that it "looks" like the family, having adequate representation of all generations, both genders, in-laws, active and passive owners, hometown and geographically distant relatives. The family council typically meets a few times each year for one or two days each time. The expenses for such a meeting may be taken care of by the family council itself.

Families in business need to nurture members' feelings of trust and pride concerning the family and business as well as build a sense of teamwork to keep a family committed and disciplined in its relationship to the business. It is wise, therefore, in the family council and family assembly to emphasize consensus decisions around family goals and policies, openness to various viewpoints, as well as significant transparency in company operations, decision making, and ownership holdings. If the family is reluctant to engage in the discussions it needs to have in the family council or assembly—out of concern about potential family conflict, not understanding what these groups should do or just being shy in these meetings—hire a facilitator to help organize the meetings. Good structures that do not address the right topics are a costly waste of time.

I want to point out again that a family council. or family assembly complements rather than replaces the board of directors. The family council sets policy for the family and recommends policy that concerns the family to the board, such as around family employment in the business. The board of directors sets policy for the business and may also make recommendations to the family council in matters that concern the business.

The board and family council should coordinate their work and not overstep each other's domains. Coordination may take the simple form of having the council and board updates each other's periodically on their important objectives, having an annual joint planning session, or having a board member sit on the council or vice versa. Again, I opt for the least complicated solution to achieve adequate communication and coordination between these two groups. In the CD group, the General Manager and the head of Finance and Accounts are invited to present the business status to the family council in the first half of the day of meeting and leave the meeting for the family members to ponder over.

The family constitution articulates a family's vision for itself and the business, its core values and the policies and guidelines that maintain family discipline. Among the policies a family council might create include:

- Employment standards for the next generation.
- Career development policies for family employees.
- Family compensation.
- Succession process, including retirement ages.
- Ownership, including buy-sell agreements.
- Dividends.

Because each of these topics, except ownership, is clearly business policy areas, the family council would consult with the board and get the board's endorsement of the policy before it becomes official. Typically, the family council also gets the approval of the family assembly before issuing a policy for the family.

Treating the family in a more formal, organizational way can feel a bit strange at first. It may take a year or two for the family to grow into this more structured way of interacting. But the value of this process is demonstrated in the strides so many families have made with these structures. They have learnt that in discussing issues that can be sensitive and raise complicated feelings, a little structure is a family's best friend.

Summary

This chapter dealt in detail about the need and importance of having family governance in place for families which are actively involved in business, business processes and decision making. The role of the family member in business and their boundaries between family and business management is crucial for business to run smoothly. The continuum of family governance structure in terms of simple to complex decision-making process, family composition (size of the family at different time periods) and stages of meeting is enumerated through a simple illustration through a figure. There are several ways of managing a family governance is discussed such as regular informal meetings with the next generation, periodical meetings, family council meetings and the importance of family constitution etc, are discussed.

References

1. Barbara Darttand, Anne Hargrave(2016), *Getting Started with Family Governance*, https://www.thefbcg.com/getting-started-with-family-governance/

2. *The Three Components of Family Governance* (2011) https://hbswk.hbs.edu/item/the-three-components-of-family-governance)

3. Dyer, W. G. (2019), "*The family edge: How your biggest competitive advantage in business isn't what you've been taught—it's your family*". Sanger, CA: Familius.

Chapter 7

Family Health and Wellness

Introduction

The chapter on health and wellness gained importance when I was discussing a number of regular authors and some family business clients about the chapter planning. I figured out that not much of a literature or research has been done in the family business domain about the health of the family members. I and my family were under Covid-19 lockdown in India, close to 45 days. I was continuing my consulting work online with the clients. But I started realizing that slowly the anxiety is growing as the pandemic syndrome continues to be in an uncertain time period. My children though were able to cope up with the online classes and unbroken learning at home all the time, there are anxious moments for them on their future of education. We, as a family had discussed a lot during our dinner time, sharing the importance of health during the pandemic period. Later I realized that I should check with the clients on what or how they are doing about their anxiety on health and business. I understood after talking to them that there is angst among the first or second generation entrepreneurs on what would be the future and how the next generation would take it further about the business; it is more to do with how to stay healthy. I realized the importance of health and wellness among the family members and it is the time to bring the awareness among the business families on wellness.

The following article is published by *Prof. Peter Vogel, Professor of Family Business and Entrepreneurship and holder of the Debiopharm Chair for Family Philanthropy, Institute for Management Development (IMD), Switzerland.* The title of the article is: A healthy family enterprise is a balancing act". I got permission to reproduce this full article as it sets the tone for the importance of health and wellness. Since Prof. Vogel, contribution through this article is significant, I reproduce without any editing. Later part I will cover the wellness part to substantiate the need for health and wellness in family business.

A Healthy Family Enterprise is a Balancing Act. (Vogel, 2020).

It is estimated that family-controlled businesses make up approximately two-thirds of the world's businesses. Their impact on global GDP and job creation is commensurate with this statistic. And yet, only 30% of family-owned businesses make it through the second generation. Through our years of experience researching and working closely with business-owning families, we found that the most successful and long-lasting family businesses focus on five areas of health and well-being: individual, family, ownership, businesses well as society and environment.

1. Personal Health and Well-Being

Individual family members need to maintain their physical and mental health, if they are to contribute to the business and the wider family enterprise system in a meaningful way. Health isn't just staying out of the hospital; it includes good nutrition and staying active through sports and other physical activities. Many families even hire advisors to support their health and well-being.

Ignoring one's individual health could have serious consequences for a business. Take the case of a hands-on family CEO and patriarch/matriarch who has led his or her family business to success and continues to control day-to-day decisions. If this person falls ill, the entire business could crumble.

Feisal Alibhai was successfully running his globally operating family business when, at the age of 35, he was diagnosed with stage-three cancer. In minutes, he handed over the business so that he could focus on survival. His experience led him to found Qineticare, the world's first family health office, helping other families proactively protect, manage and improve their quality of health and wellbeing.

Indeed, "if you aren't well on the inside then you can't be a good leader", John Elkann, Chairman of Fiat Chrysler Automobiles, once famously said.

2. A Healthy Family Unit

Family harmony, trust, unity and more generally healthy relationships across the family are crucial aspects for achieving generational continuity and ensuring family enterprise longevity. Clear family governance in areas of conflict management, decision-making and feedback, all based on the alignment of family values, and is essential.

There are countless high-profile cases of family feuds that have not only ripped apart the enterprising family but also disrupted the business. No matter if it's the Koch brothers' famous legal fight back in the 80s and 90s, or the legal action taken by Frank Stronach, the billionaire founder of Magna. He sued his daughter Belinda, his handpicked successor and the current chair and president of The Stronach Group (as well as her children and others) in the Ontario Superior Court for $520 million. This was for alleged misappropriation of company funds and for locking him out of the family's horse racing and betting empire. The case was settled in late January 2020. But the damage was done.

The enterprising family should establish a clear family vision articulating what they would like to achieve together.

3. Healthy Family Enterprise Ownership

Having an ownership group that is emotionally connected, well-informed and capable of taking responsible decisions – in the interests of the various stake holder groups – is a major asset of family enterprises. However, that requires strong ownership governance, discipline and an open and collaborative exchange between the owners.

One of the key advantages of family-controlled businesses is a highly concentrated ownership structure, allowing for effective and efficient decision-making in times of change. However, if the ownership group's decision-making ability is impaired by conflicts or other challenges, it can stifle the business.

Healthy ownership means that there is a clear ownership vision and strategy for the organization, which takes into account the family's values as well as the business needs and priorities. Owners come to act as stewards to the business, its employees and its customers. The task of budding the next generation of responsible owners who feel a sense of duty and responsibility, but also privilege and pride, is critical. Allowing them growing into a position of being emotionally connected to the legacy business is of vital importance.

Healthy ownership also takes a more long-term and "patient" approach, trying to stay away from what is sometimes called the "shiny object syndrome" that is getting distracted or lured into short-term achievements, neglecting the big picture.

4. Organizational Performance

Running a high-performing and profitable business is essential for enterprising families – especially if they are growing in size over time – to ensure wealth preservation and ideally, growth.

Running a high-performing business requires disciplined leadership and management and world-class governance on all levels – ownership, board and top management. It is essential that these different levels know exactly what it is they are supposed to do vis-à-vis the other levels. Having a clear definition of roles and responsibilities of owners, board members and the top management team is paramount to ensure long-term success.

Other essential factors include, but are not limited to strategic foresight, innovativeness, financial excellence, as well as a strong talent management and succession planning – both family and non-family talents.

In view of performance or times of transformation it is also of critical importance that family businesses are both resilient and adaptable. It is resilient, because they will need to hold on to their long-term plans and strategies. Adaptable, because they will need to embrace agile and entrepreneurial traits, scan the market environment and understand the big global trends that might affect their industry and become a threat to their very existence.

5. Societal and Environmental Impact

A growing number of today's enterprising families want to leverage their assets as a force for good endorsement. It can be a tough choice to de-invest from the core business, but many family enterprises are doing it. Another approach that we are seeing is that a growing number of enterprising families are re-evaluating their core business models and start transforming them into more purpose-driven ones.

Why? The old model – embodied by historic business moguls like John D. Rockefeller – saw entrepreneurs getting rich on businesses that were often harmful to the environment or society, like oil, and then using their philanthropy to offset the harmful effects of their activities. It was akin to committing a 'sin' and then confessing in church.

Today, this mindset is passé. Businesses have for some time now been de-investing from many of the most harmful industries. Leaders are finally focused on doing less harm and doing better through activities like advocacy, impact investing, corporate social responsibility, sustainable development goals and philanthropy.

A good balance between these separate layers is just as important to helping the family enterprise system flourish across generations as good leadership at the top.

Wellness

Definition of Wellness

Wellness is an active process of becoming aware of and making choices toward a healthy and fulfilling life. Wellness is more than being free from illness; it is a dynamic process of change and growth.

"A state of complete physical, mental and social well-being and not merely the absence of disease or infirmity"

Stated by
World Health Organization (WHO)

In order to maintain a higher quality of life, knowing and understanding *wellness* is crucial. Our state of mind or well-being directly affects our actions and emotions. Therefore, it is important for everyone to achieve optimal wellness in order to be free from stress, reduce the risk of illness and ensure positivity itself, interaction with others and in the relationships.

According to WHO[2], the common health problem in the world is depression and 256 million people across the world are affected by depression. This problem is often manifested in the form of insomnia, stress, poor nutrition, physical inactivity, obesity, and heart disease, etc. Depression is a psycho-somatic disorder and results in sickness of the body. It requires medical treatment and sometimes needs a psychological therapy depending on the intensity of it. Stress on the other hand is very common among people due to pressure from the work and economic conditions. While these psychosomatic disorders play havoc in the health of the individual, it is important for us to understand the concept of wellness as defined by WHO.

Wellness is the conscious development of the whole self. Embarking on a wellness journey is a process of searching for the appropriate "tools" to make you a healthier and happier human being, together with discovering your own effective methods to use these "tools" for continued growth and development. As there is a great variety on all aspects of life, there are also countless ways to cultivate you on an ever-changing path of wellness.

Family Business and Wellness

The family businesses need to focus on the wellness aspects of all its members. The reason, radical shift is happening in the demographic variables. My understanding has increased over last few years of those demographical changes by the personal experiences and by reading. Further, number of families live with their grandparents and they take care of the grandchildren and vice versa. The life span increase also throws another challenge as the founders or the leaders of the business from the family tend to spend longer years in the business while the younger generations grow and find no space for risk and decision making. They get frustrated that the older generations though talk about succession planning, they are unwilling to hand over the powers and things to let go.

The changing family demographics and more elderly people in the home, and younger one's postponements of their marriages and associated problems, with the pollutions causing additional health issues, the family businesses must focus on the health of the each of the family member.

Family and Wellness

We discussed in detail, the family constitution in the 5th chapter. Families must think of writing **wellness** as one of the important areas to focus. The constitution should talk not only about education, qualification to step into the family business, but also wellness as the criteria. In India we often say "*sound body sound mind*" that denotes the connection between body and mind and its importance to focus on wellness.

There is a Tamil verse reciting;

Udambaar aliyin…

When the body is in decay

Life will be in decay. And they would never

Reach the centre of wisdom; I,

Learning the art of preserving health

Learned health, wellness and breathe…

Thirumoolar.

The famous story which I heard during my college days, about the Ambani brothers as they famously know, sons of the founder of Reliance Group of Industries Dhirubhai Ambani, was a remarkable one. Years before he died, told his younger son, **Anil**: "Look Son, you can buy any luxury you want in life -- from clothes to food, from a home to a holiday -- but you can never buy health. Do whatever it takes to make you feel good." The younger Ambani was touching 40 then. He weighed an uncomfortable 105 kg and could barely walk a kilometer in an hour, let alone run. Like his father, his fitness, or rather lack of it, also had his shareholders worried[3]. Rest is history how he became a marathon runner and known as fitness freak. It is a classic example of how the businessmen should take care of the health so that they can confidently take the business forward and investors would look at them as best bet for investments.

I wanted to share one more story on the positive impact of health practice. One of my clients explained in the previous chapters called CD Group, where two brothers manage the family business. The younger brother Shanmugasundaram (Shan) is a great example of fitness and family health practice. He was weighing 94 Kgs 2 years ago, had disc *prolapse* and had a great difficulty in even standing for over 5 minutes continuously. It was really taking a toll on his business and personal life. He couldn't make his business travels and attend social gatherings.

He decided that if something is not done about this, it would ruin his life and the family's happiness. He did go to few doctors and did all kinds of medical tests. That is when he came across the weight losing diet program and got interested in it as his brother Mr. Kumar benefitted by practicing the same. He shared the following while I was listening to his story of fitness;

> *I still remember the day I visited the dietician, the shirt I was wearing, the button in the belly area, was about to pop out. The dietician's fee was a hefty one. But, the thought of the recurrence of the back pain made me bite the bullet. Ever since then, there was no looking back". In the midway of the diet program, my dietician suggested that I start walking. I started walking for just 5 minutes, this moved to 10, 15, 30, and 45 and now I do about a minimum of 60 minutes. First, I increased my duration and then started working on my pace. I also started using some Apps to tack my progress. I hired a personal trainer to help me strengthen my core muscles. I shared by progress with my friends and family. A lot of them appreciated and encouraged me. There were a few of my friends who were inspired by me and started walking or working out. This gave me a sense of satisfaction.*

Today, I am 69.5 Kgs

I also realised that our employees were also noticing the change in my physical appearance. Our General Manager, on a few occasions, when talking to customers, would bring them to my room and tell them that I had reduced about 15 Kgs and that they should also take care of their health too taking me as an example and inspiration. One of our big customers started walking and realised the importance of health.

Among my Family members, relatives and employees, I am looked at as a person to follow in terms of Good Health. I try to prevail upon my family members to eat healthy, exercise and have a good sleep. During the early stages of COVID-19 lockdown, our entire family (4 Generations) was walking for at least 45 minutes daily in the evening, gaining inspiration from me.

My biggest learning is, when we walk the talk, our stake holders take us seriously and their approach to us changes for the better. As a leader, it is my responsibility to be physically and mentally fit. I feel, leading by example is one of the best forms of leadership.

The elder generations in the family also needs to pay lots of attention as gerontological issues can harm them in paying attention to details in business. In order to run the business and guide the younger generations the older people in the family must focus on their healthy diets and if possible, some physical workouts.

While one focus on the wellness, it is also important that there is sufficient coverage in terms any sickness. Families must have managers or health insurance advisors to advise the family business on insurance covers. The Constitution must say that annual health checkup is must for everyone after some years of age that may be defined.

Family Business and Employees

The employees, who work in family businesses need to be protected as they are the workforce, need to be hale and healthy. Family businesses must protect their employees by opting for the schemes such as Employees' State Insurance Scheme, which is offered by the Government of India.

The Employees' State Insurance Scheme is an integrated measure of Social Insurance embodied in the Employees' State Insurance Act and it is designed to accomplish the task of protecting **'employees'** as defined in the **Employees' State Insurance Act, 1948** against the impact of incidences of sickness, maternity, disablement and death due to employment injury and to provide medical care to insured persons and their families. These kinds of schemes are good measures for the family businesses to extend a good cover of the health for the employees and protection for the owners of the family firms.

Many of the Asian countries such as South Korea, Thailand, Indonesia, The Philippines and others have government and private insurance schemes for the firms which employ certain number of employees.

Good Nutrition and Staying Active

Good nutrition is a common and universal idea sometimes differs with reference to the conditions of living, age and region. In Earlier times common sense told us that eating much food especially, Non vegetarian variety could provide much health, but that it is not the case, food is a sensitive item which should have its limits and more to do with the culture, living style and place of living. Here in Tamilnadu or south India we now try to have our traditional food including millets. European food intake may be different, also the Chinese, Japanese food varieties. Millets have proved to be a healthy food, so much close to our living style as well as traditional. Millets prove to be good for all ages too. Beef is a common food among non-tropical nations which is full of protein. Food has been invented by human beings through their best choice of eating practices enhanced by empirical ways. Individuals know what to eat, what is good for their health but their body would need a change of food whilst aging or affected conditions. Then they require the help of a medical practitioner or counselor. Good food, fitness practices and enough rest all would ensure a health to an individual.

Family Harmony

Family harmony is an important factor ensuring stability to any family business, giving longevity and ensuring steady line of products moving to the market. When a family is intact it shows trust and selflessness is practiced among them. This characterization is important for a business to attain its goal and exercising creative nuances in due course which in return would give it a thrust to face any stiff competency. Harmony gives peace and the living home becomes a serene atmosphere which will not spoil thinking, which in return would give innovative ideas to flourish. Harmony among members in a family also results in getting individual support from the family members which would reduce conflict. In a conflict reduced atmosphere business or any idea may get its shape with a collective consciousness, there too working with harmonious, emotionally cohering minds. Further, if any key person operating business is sick on a temporary or long duration on chronic illnesses another one can give support both in business as well as curing illness, nursing him. Family members can take him to destinations of healthcare with no annoyance.

Discipline: Strong Ownership in Governance

Discipline is a much sought-after characterization for an individual to move ahead on his routines and maintaining health. Our body is designed in the way it requires certain feedback like food, water, and sleep on prescribed times. The body clock works all 24 hours to keep it fit for all conflict and non-conflict timings and it has its own intelligence. We talk about herd immunity which may protect against epidemics; solely are ideas and information designed by our bodies to protect any foreign body invasion. Our cells get alien messages and try to understand them and protect our body with the help of soldier cells; the TCELLS. When this design is so long inherent in us we need not worry about how an illness is caused and how it is cured too!!!

Doing things which suits to our body, that is regular fitness programs, early wake up from bed, having enough food but limited in the breakfast, correct tables of eating, having pleasant ideas in mind and relaxation at the time of rest all would turn out to be the bounty that we have to keep it all through our lives which will result in STRONG OWNERSHIP IN GOVERNANCE.

Harmful to the Environment

A good family must think righteous deeds that would help society and human beings' wealth that could be trusted and saved for generations but also for the society. In Tamilnadu Amalgamation group has wound up its business long back but it has a name behind that. It never ventured into any business which is harmful for society and individuals. An investment on toxic substance production or prowling the natural resources may sometimes yield profit on a temporary momentum but in the long run could have exhausted natural resource and so also will not ensure any life security for the future generations; that would only see the end of a livelihood in that region. Health is not just about the health of the members of the business family alone rather it is the health of the environment and the health of the workers involved in the business and health of the flora, fauna and human beings live around the industry.

Summary

We have so far discussed key issues and factors influencing family business in simpler understandable terms that may help a reader picking up points in a nutshell as a ready inventory. I have not provided any long list of tasks rather few tasks alone if anyone could adapt himself within the realm of families involved in business it may fructify well and virtuous. These lines which I discuss would fall within a scientific purview and not merely speculative.

This is a work that has come out of an inspiration from me and my long stint of experiences with families and businesses. So, trust me and be with me on my sessions that I may vouch to give you enlightened on what we aspire to: **MAKE ONE FAMILY DOING FANTASTIC BUSINESS.**

References

1. *Peter Vogel (2020), "A healthy family enterprise is a balancing act". Professor of Family Business and Entrepreneurship and holder of the Debiopharm Chair for Family Philanthropy, Institute for Management Development (IMD), Switzerland.*

2. www.who.int

3. https://www.rediff.com/getahead/slide-show/slide-show-1-specials-india-s-super-toned-billionaires/20130304.htm

Case Study

URC Construction Company (URCC), incorporated in 1956, is a national contractor and flagship company of the URC Group. The construction company was originally started by Mr. UR Chinnusamy as a first-generation entrepreneur. Shri U.R. Chinnusamy kick started it as a small contractor undertaking and supervising the construction of irrigation systems. Head quartered in Erode, Tamil Nadu, and URC Construction is a major player in South India has also branched out in the north and other parts of India. It is the flagship company of the group. With a rich heritage and an exhaustive and diverse portfolio of successfully completed projects across industry sectors, the company is poised for the next era of growth. The key factors to its robust and stable growth are its client focus, its leadership, the adoption of the latest technology and its work force orientation. URCC brings a host of capabilities to major infrastructure projects through an integrated approach that spans the life cycle of infrastructure to professional & support services. Today, the company is a leader and a trendsetter in the construction industry, delivering custom-designed turnkey projects to government agencies, large corporations and private bodies.

The company has many portfolios and successfully completed several projects. In the 1950s and 60s, the company started out work with several public sector projects such as the construction of canals, dams, irrigation and power projects. In the late 60s, URC entered mass housing projects. The 80s saw the second generation entering the business and had aspirations to take the company to different verticals and progress. The next level leaders forayed into institutional buildings, construction of factories, facilities for core sector industries such as sugar, education and textiles. The early 90s was a period of consolidation and organization. It was also when the group entered the Oil & Chemical sector. This followed the acquisition of heavy machinery to boost assets. URC engaged technical and management consultants to sustain its growth and gear up the progress further from the year 2000, assuming the need for modernization and new thinking.

Mr. U R Chinnusamy and his wife Ms. C Thulasiammal have two sons and one daughter. Mr. Kanagasabapathy is the first son married to Ms. K. Saraswathi and Mr. Devarajan is the second son married to Ms. D. Kamlam. Ms. Devi is the daughter and married to Mr. Palanisamy, who is also inducted into the company as a director of the company. Mr. Kanagasabpathy is current chairman and mostly spends time in managing the school from the family trust, involves and manages all CSR initiatives and projects of the company. Mr. Devarajan is the Managing Director of the company along with Mr. Palanisamy; he takes care of all the Metro Rail projects across the country and any projects generally in Karnataka. Mr. Devarajan, on the other hand drives all the verticals especially the projects in core industries sector, across the nation. Also, Devarajan is the front face of the company and mainly focuses on Public Relations and Branding. Around 2010, the third generations entered the business and currently driving the business to the next level in all opportunities in construction business. Currently, the company turnover is USD 130 million, with 1300 employees and 7000 indirect workers, operating in 11 states in India. The third generation has an ambition of reaching 1billion USD business in next 5 years period.

URC family business is an interesting case study for the people who are looking for some learning from the family business management. Mr. U R Chinnusamy, included the daughter in the business contrary to the general practice in the region. Later, the son in law is also brought into the system. However, the business is divided among the brothers and sister geographically and in some places sector wise responsibilities are shared in between them to have better control and growth. The first brother didn't have any sons and have only two daughters, therefore, he moved away from the main business activities to take care of the philanthropically related projects of the family. Ms. Devi, the daughter moved to Bangalore and started expanding the business along with her husband Mr. Palanisamy.

Mr. Devarajan, who stayed back in the roots and spent longer time with his father and mentor in the business and life, took care of the business in Tamilnadu initially and expanded to different geographical locations and sectors.

I had an interview with Mr. Devarajan for writing a case study for this book and his learning from the father, and his dreams for the business and second generations. He met me in the year 2005, when I was heading an OB department in a leading business school in Mysore and invited me as an OD consultant for his company to help growing to next level. We designed and implemented interventions that moved the company from USD 8 million business to USD 35 million. Later, with the other group consultants and a stalwart Mr. A Ramakrishnan, retired managing Director of L&T, the largest construction company in India, and the company moved to new heights.

I requested Mr. Devarajan about my ambition of writing a book and including his family and company as a case study. He readily agreed and the excerpts are given below, taken only from the family business perspectives:

Mohanakrishnan (MK): Mr. Devarajan Thanks for giving consent to this interview and it is nice to see the current level of growth of your company. I know you are a second-generation entrepreneur and have taken the company to the next level. I am also aware that you have a lovely and caring family at the same time very disciplined one too. I like to know some of your experiences of managing the family members and the business.

C Devarajan (CD): Thanks, Mohanakrishnan. My best wishes for the book and I am glad to present this interview to you. We worked closely for close to 5 years and later again for 3 years for the group. As you know, the value system of my father was that none of his brood suffers or leads a stressful life. He wanted to see us as a happy and stress-free family with this business and the accumulated wealth. So, for me initially to convince him on the importance of growth was a tough part. I took very careful steps to gain his confidence to move forward.

MK: can you narrate some of the interesting learning from your father?

CD: He strongly believed that "Business is the means of life, not the purpose of life and one should have larger purpose in life". His all actions in the family, including business centred on that. He saw business as a means and he had higher priority for people around him, especially for the employees, never hesitated to support them anytime there was a need. He believed in values such as care for people, relationships, and in giving back to the society. Even today, if you look at our business or family we practice this sincerely in all domains.

MK: How did you learn these values from him, did you have any systems of learning from the elders or from the father as a founder?

CD: No, we did not even know that there was a need to have such systems. It was part of our culture and credit goes to my mother, who is the pivotal point of holding all family members together. We have been taught or being insisted to sit with them for the breakfast and dinner to share how the day is going to be and, in the dinner, to share what happened on that day. So, it became a habit of sharing mutually and my father used to share lots of his experiences too each day. And it became a habit with everyone.

MK: it is interesting and obviously I am curious to know this knowledge or values are transferred to the third generation, like your son Kabilan?

CD: My son was taken care of most of the time by my parents at home, and he used to spend more time with the grandparents than me as he was young. I was busy with projects which demanded lots of travel. So, in a way, my son is the most beneficiary of learning from my father. Kabilan used to ask so many questions with my father and inculcated and imbibed the values which are traditional from my father. Now, it is my desire that I should spend more time and share the experiences and stories to my grandchildren.

MK: This is amazing, and I see the learning goes as it is part of life and gets communicated to generation to generation, without setting any learning systems for learning values and best practices of the family in business. How do you propose to engage with your grandchildren to pass on your learning to them?

CD: I strongly believe that children observe everything about the parents. They understand what kind of conversations we have at homes among the family members. I observed in my young age that whatever has been spoken is being practiced. There was no ambiguity or conflict in what is being spoken and behaved. This is important for children to learn from the parents and I propose to do the same with my children.

MK: Would you recall any one big challenge faced by you or the company and how your family was able to stand by you? Meaning how family facilitates the firm's performance?

CD: This is a very interesting question. The answer I am going to give is a self-righteous one not only for me but for the whole URC family. We have secured one of the largest valuable projects, around 800 crores in Bangalore, Karnataka. It is building a metro rail project along with another big player in the market as a JV partner. We won the contract with the agreement from the bankers that they will supply the bank guarantee. But later the JV company had some challenges in producing necessary documents to the bank and we were in a situation we might lose the project. Because the bank was demanding documents for collateral purpose which was completely lagging behind and becoming impossible from the Strategic Business Unit (SBU) -2, as we call it. For practical and effective management, we have made three SBUs within the construction group. This Metro rail project was the prestigious and largest in our company history and we decided not to lose the project. Since the tender was won by the SBU-2 (managed by me and my son) and challenges were posed on to us; we were at crossroads and didn't know how to proceed further. The challenges were shared to the family and all directors involved in solving the issue. As a family we all stood together and decided that all three families will pitch in for collaterals for the bank. In any other situation, the family would not have given those properties as collateral but for the unity of the family and the business or organization's success. I emphasize that business families when they confront such a situation should come to the table and do the analysis, all pros and cons and decide how the apt decision will help the organization and demonstrate the family unity. I am indebted to the whole family having stood by me to win the project and successful completion of the project.

MK: What is the most important character of your family and that is reflected in business and goes as a lesson to all employees?

CD: I strongly believe in "what I say, I must do; and I must do what I say". Today our company is grown to a greater height because of this character. We never came out of any projects due to conflicts with the client, never compromised on quality of construction and never backed out due to delayed payments or challenges in collecting our money from the client. We always complete the project to the end and come out with utmost satisfaction. If you look at our receivables, you may wonder how we manage the business. We had tough times, but we carried on with the business due to the value systems which flowed from the founder. But these value systems are the ones that gave lots of good name and good will, customer retention and referral projects and more. Therefore, I want to ensure that there is no difference in family and business practice. We consider the employees are also as a part of the family. Employees observe us and they practice. That's my experience with them.

MK: You engaged me for close to 5 years and again for 3 years later. I also know that you engaged a big consulting firm in construction domain. Why do you invest and invite consultants?

CD: We invite consultants to learn from outside the company what the best practices are and to get critical and objective views from them. They bring new energy and new insights. It is worth learning and getting help from the experts outside the company. We benefitted a lot from them.

MK: Do you have anything to share for other family businesses in your region or in general?

CD: Sure. The founder of any company starts with a purpose. This purpose needs to be understood clearly by the successive generations and along with the encircled values of the purpose. Then the culture of the company needs to be built around this purpose and values. Also, the current generation which manages the business must think and build an institution to live longer for the many more generations to come.

MK: Thanks for your time and it is valuable lessons I learned from you. My best wishes to you and your family for further success.

CD: Thanks, Mohanakrishnan. I also wish you the best in bringing out a useful volume in family business.

Learning Points

The above interview was on many other topics, but I picked what is relevant to this book's context. According to me there are few definite ideas to take into account:

1. The relationship between the father and the sons, is imperative for smooth transitioning of the learning, values and culture,
2. The first-generation parents build a home with a congenial environment for their children to learn from the parents, freely able to share and ask questions to know, learn and understand,
3. Family Values drive the business organization to the most,
4. Learn through vicarious learning,
5. Have a higher purpose in life, have a dream and desire to carry forward the business to several generations.

Concluding Comments By the Author

Whilst I end this work with a note that is quoted from the scriptures, 'in the beginning is the end' I remind any family business should start with a commercial plan imbibed with a value which throws responsibility over the world or society which in turn would make the venture an *everlasting* and *esteemed* one. It should start with a writing, I may say the writing giving a spotlight, that would give energy and efficiency. Togetherness is a maxim exercised in history in the name of *mutual aid* and *team spirit*. And the team spirit must be cemented with *reciprocity*. This may make wonders that small would become big, in cutting across the greatest layers of time. Like the seeds of all tress are small but have the potential to grow large, a business is oriented to family which stands as a mark of tree, both have branches, root and a strong stem. The stem is the business strategy brought on by the mechanism of togetherness. Read this work and respond me any time.

MOHANAKRISHNAN RAMAN

www.ingramcontent.com/pod-product-compliance
Lightning Source LLC
Chambersburg PA
CBHW030647220526

45463CB00005B/1664